Missing Alice

WRITING AMERICAN WOMEN

Carol A. Kolmerten, *Series Editor*

Hunter College Senior, Alice Parson.
New York City, 1932.

Missing

IN SEARCH OF A
MOTHER'S VOICE

Alice

SUSAN

LETZLER

COLE

SYRACUSE UNIVERSITY PRESS

Syracuse University Press, Syracuse, New York 13244–5160

Copyright © 2007 by Susan Letzler Cole
All Rights Reserved

First Edition 2007
07 08 09 10 11 12   6 5 4 3 2 1

For a listing of books published and distributed by Syracuse University Press,
visit our Web site at SyracuseUniversityPress.syr.edu.

Excerpt of poem by Marya Bradley in Part 4
reprinted with permission of the author.

All photographs courtesy of author.

ISBN-13: 978–0–8156–0864–6   ISBN-10: 0–8156–0864–0

Library of Congress Cataloging-in-Publication Data
Cole, Susan Letzler, 1940–
Missing Alice : in search of a mother's voice / Susan Letzler Cole.
p. cm.—(Writing American women)
Includes bibliographical references.
ISBN-13: 978–0–8156–0864–6 (cloth : alk. paper)
ISBN-10: 0–8156–0864–0 (cloth : alk. paper)
1. Mothers and daughters. I. Title.
HQ759.C685 2007
306.874'3—dc22
2007000342

Manufactured in the United States of America

For
Alice Parson Letzler

ὦ φθέγμ᾽, ἀφίκου;

Susan Letzler Cole is the author of *The Absent One: Mourning Ritual, Tragedy, and the Performance of Ambivalence* (Pennsylvania State University Press); *Directors in Rehearsal: A Hidden World* (Routledge); and *Playwrights in Rehearsal: The Seduction of Company* (Routledge). She is a professor of English and director of the concentration in creative writing at Albertus Magnus College. She lives in New Haven with her husband, playwright David Cole.

Contents

Illustrations

Acknowledgments

I AM DEEPLY GRATEFUL for the advice, support, and generosity of the following: Sky Avila, Sr. Ann Bailie, O.P., Scott Bartlett, Peg Blumenthal, Marya Bradley, Kathleen Collins, William Combs, Peter Detre, María Helena Dolan, Cai Emmons, Claire Finkelstein, Deborah Frattini, Elinor Fuchs, Carrie Horvath, Greg Knobelsdorff, Jacqueline Kozin, Julie Lee, Ron Lee, Ben Letzler, Kenneth Letzler, Robert Letzler, John Leubsdorf, Beverly Mack, Sharon Magnarelli, Alice Mattison, Carolyn McCarthy, Edward Moran, Milton Moss, Lucille ("Buffy") Parson, Patti Parson, Dr. William Parson, Chris Powell, Marc Robinson, Eric Schoeck, Sylvia Shuey, Amy Swauger, Bea Taruskin, Carol Tennessen, Magda Teter, and Kathleen Woodward. I especially want to offer thanks to Garrett Dell, Meg Gertmenian, Amie Keddy, Natalie Miller, and Susan Schorr.

I am particularly indebted to Glenn Wright and Carol Kolmerten at Syracuse University Press for their enthusiastic support of this project.

In various stages of production, the book profited from the careful attention of Lynn Hoppel, Lisa Kuerbis, Victoria Lane, Theresa Litz, Kay Steinmetz, Therese Walsh, and Ann Youmans.

Finally, I want to thank my husband, David Cole, whose tireless close reading of successive drafts, astonishing wisdom, and unfailing love have made all things possible.

Preface

MY MOTHER'S VOICE is one of the voices we're losing in the world. Vanishing ahead of us is a generation of women who came of age during the Depression, gave birth during the last world war, did not greet the millennium with their children. Most of them are un-celebrated, undocumented, hardly remarked upon as they pass from our view. These women made a life out of certain values that contribute much to the world we have known. We need to listen to more of them: old voices, sick voices, quiet voices.

Alice's voice is musical and well-modulated with an intelligence that lives in its varied patterns of stresses and rhythms. Recognizably feminine, it is a voice of many colors and lights. There is, surprisingly, no trace of her native New York in her accent. It is a voice in the medium range, sometimes falling into the lower range. Except when tired or nervous or saddened by a particular memory, her voice carries a sense of pleasure in all the sounds of every word it knows. There is a nearly poetic sense of prose rhythm in its emphases, a hint that the sounds of a voice in conversation can be as musically precise as those of poetry. Saying "fifty-three," the voice takes pleasure in the strong "r" of "three"; "snow" is caressed in the phrase "in the snow," and "deep" in the phrase "in this deep snow." Always distinct, never loud, never shrill, Alice's voice avoids the contemporary rising inflection at the ends of sentences and phrases. There is nothing lazy or inattentive in the wordsounds it sings in conversation or in its flawless command of grammar and syntax. This voice is not in the least showy. Anyone who is attentive to the music of speech would recognize its quality.

Alice's voice was my earliest connection with her. It is what I miss most. Photographs won't return it; dreams can't reproduce it. My aural memories require a reappearance of sound, and now there is silence. None of us can be counted on to be always fully present in the voice. But she was, with me. In the sounds of our voices, we didn't hide or withdraw from the other. Voice was our most intimate emotional, intellectual, and spiritual meeting place. My mother was fully alive, uniquely present, in her voice. I have never heard anything like it.

Introduction

THE TRUTH WE ALL KNOW and rarely speak is that mourning the loss of those we love has no closure.

Does it help us to know this? I think it does. Death can end much, but it cannot end our conversation with the dead, a conversation that returns on its own rhythms and renews itself, in memory and dreams, in speech and in silence. Our relationships with the dead we have loved are in the present tense.

Missing Alice: In Search of a Mother's Voice is an experimental memoir, the autobiography of two voices. Alice Parson Letzler died of colon cancer in the late summer of 1990 at the age of seventy-eight; three summers later, I began to write a series of letters to her that appear in part 1 of this book. But *her* voice was missing. The year before my mother died, she and I had made three tapes: an unfinished "oral history" of her life. For the first time since her death, I listened to, and then transcribed, those tapes. Our conversation from the past became part 2 of this book—what I thought then was its conclusion, the end of my search for my mother's voice.

The following summer, I discovered in the bottom of a file cabinet in my brother's basement a small notebook covered in brown wrapping paper. It said, "Property of Alice Parson. Private." On the second page were the words "Diary: Memoirs, Comments, Incidents." I hesitated, and then I began reading.

Alice's diary was written in July and August 1926 when she was fourteen and her own mother had suddenly and mysteriously fallen ill, though she did recover. It contains a voice I never heard—so very young, plucky, dutiful, at times bewildered, always hopeful. But the adolescent diary is opaque, the diarist hidden in her diary. In part 3, I again write letters to a missing Alice, a fourteen-year-old diarist, the mother who isn't there yet. Finally, in part 4, I write my own diary: I write myself.

What are the narrative strategies appropriate to the project of telling a life? The obvious way to tell a life is a chronological account, with a beginning, middle, and end. My project is different. I begin by writing to my mother, not about her. I don't re-present the events of her life as she had lived them. The "text" is a series of texts, a collaboration between a dead mother and a living daughter, a collaboration in which my mother "speaks" and "writes" herself into this book.

In my search for my mother's voice, I find the voice of a lost daughter. In my search for my mother's voice, I find my own.

Writing to my mother I meet her again. Death cannot sever a relationship in the present tense.

Because what follows is not a chronological account of her life, here are some "facts" I know about my mother. Born in New York City on May 16, 1912, Alice Parson was the daughter of immigrant Jewish parents: her father, Morris Kalman Parson (the last name had been changed, possibly from "Perchick," at Ellis Island), was born in 1874 in Minsk, Russia; her mother, Anna Levitt, born in 1878, was from Grodno. My mother was the middle child and only daughter in the family. Her half brother Rudy was eight years older; her brother Bill, a year and a half younger. The family first lived in the Bronx where Kalman Parson owned a small delicatessen. When Alice was twelve, her father bought what was called a "candy store" (though it sold more than candy) on the corner of Church and Argyle Streets in Brooklyn. The Parson family lived in a flat behind the store where Alice worked while she attended Erasmus Hall High School and then, as a live-at-home scholarship student, Hunter College.

Alice graduated from college in June 1932, having majored in Latin with a minor in Greek. She was barely twenty and it was the height of the Depression. She passed the tests for a New York City teaching license, but no teaching positions were to be had anywhere in the city.

Alice worked for a year cataloguing jobs in one of the organizations President Roosevelt created for people without jobs during the Depression, and then, after a short stint in a dry cleaning store, she was hired as a fourth-grade teacher in Roosevelt, Long Island, where she lived with the family of her older brother, Rudy. In 1936, Alice applied for, and was offered, a job as an examining clerk for the Civil Service Commission in Washington, D.C., at a salary of $1,440 a year. She lived on her own for the first time in her life, rooming in a Washington, D.C., boarding house where her husband-to-be, a young government attorney, also lived. On May 8, 1937, Alfred Letzler and Alice Parson were married and moved to an apartment in Arlington, Virginia. My mother accepted a position, with an increase in salary, at the newly created Social Security Board. In 1940 she gave birth to her first child, a daughter, and after a few months of maternity leave continued her work, relying on paid child-care help at home. In 1943 she gave birth to a son. At that time, it was difficult to retain the quality of child-care help she had depended on in the past, and she resigned from her position at the Social Security Board to become a full-time mother. From then until six days before her death, she was continually involved in state- and community-based work, mainly unpaid or underpaid, primarily educational and cultural, work she embraced with joy and meticulously brought to perfection.

Missing Alice is not a celebration or critique of the private life of a public figure. It is a search for the possibilities of communication in, and from, hitherto unexplored or silent places. This is the "story" it tells.

Some may find it an idealized story. My mother, like everyone else, had limitations, I suppose. Some of them bothered me; some of them didn't. In this book I engage neither those that bothered me nor those that didn't. This book is about something else.

Epilogue

October 2006

Dearest One,

This is a book made of many summers. Now autumn arrives, a season you loved. Summer for me is a welcoming, is you—and yet it is the season when both you and Dad ended your lives. My life began in summer; yours closed.

To embrace the season you loved is another way of knowing you. I find you in the subdued brilliance of these uncomplaining autumn leaves.

Missing Alice

PART I

Echolocations

A letter is a joy of Earth—
It is denied the Gods—
　　—Emily Dickinson

June 6, 1993
4:30 P.M.

Dear Alice,

I remember the box: rectangular, perhaps a shoe box once, clean cardboard, neatly filled with letters all the same size, addresses all written in the same neat clear handwriting, my father's name on the envelopes. A year before you died, you asked me to look for those letters in the attic and bring them down to you. I didn't read them, didn't think of reading them, oddly. I left you alone with them in the new room we added at the back of the house, the room where Dad had died. A few days later, after you had reread the letters my father had kept, you told me you had decided to throw them out. I remember your saying you hadn't saved his letters to you, but he had saved all yours (he saved many things: string, stubby pencils, worn clothing, old tennis balls, stamps from all over the world, the written records of his children's school work and achievements, theater programs, nails of various lengths, odd-shaped pieces of wood, cans of leftover paint, receipts, unworn ties I persisted in giving him for his birthday).

You said that these letters written when you were young didn't give a true portrait of the depth of your feelings for each other, were superficial accounts of daily events, did not convey the real nature of your life and marriage. (How could they? I now ask.) After you told me this, you asked if I would deposit the box of letters in the new black trash can on wheels by the gate to your backyard.

I didn't argue or plead. I did as you desired, believing in your right to decide the fate of your own writing. For several days, as we both knew, that box of letters sat, waiting for the garbage truck. I remember thinking that I could retrieve your letters, read them, and return them without being seen or interrogated. But that seemed a violation not only of your trust in me but of the nature of the writing itself: it was private, even if not—in some sense I didn't quite understand—"intimate," and its audience, its only audience, was now dead. On Wednesday evening, I rolled those letters to the end of the driveway and early next morning I must have heard the sounds of their being collected as trash.

Now that unopened box haunts me.

Dear Alice,

Yesterday I noticed a tiny bat hanging upside down between the window pane and the storm window on the landing below our third-floor apartment. I have never seen a baby bat up close before, but I am certain this is one. What I don't know is whether it is alive or dead. It is about two and a half inches long, with mangy, light brown fur; its head is obscured. Its "thighs" look like miniaturized black badminton rackets and its tiny toes clinging to the rim of the storm window look like a marvel of bronze sculpture. The criss-crossing lines on its black folded wings are startling in their beauty.

I am too afraid to open the window. Last night on our way to an evening walk, I showed it to my husband. David said that if the bat was smart enough to find its way in, it would know how to find its way out. I replied that if it was dumb enough to get in this awful fix, it was dumb enough not to get out of it.

It is still there today. I'm learning to be less afraid of it.

I remember one dullish afternoon when I went looking for something in the basement of your immaculate house in Virginia, the one my brother and I have now sold. There I found, to my utter surprise, a tiny brown mouse who was no less surprised by my arrival. Once, long ago, in graduate school, I had watched an actress, a friend of my roommate's, leap onto a chair and shriek with horror at the sight of such a mouse as this; years later, after the Virginia mouse, I aggravated an already painful sore throat by screaming at a startled gray mouse disappearing into a hole in my kitchen floor in New Haven.

But that afternoon in your basement, I silently surveyed the scene and reported to you upstairs. I guess I thought you would do whatever needed to be done. Instead, I saw my fear on your face. We were alone in the house. I found a large box and a shovel, and tried to direct the mouse toward the one with the other. As time passed I may have become careless in my frustration and impatience.

All I remember is that in the process of my removing the mouse to the backyard, it died, either from shock or badly aimed zeal or perhaps of natural causes. Perhaps it had come *into* the basement to die. I remember your genuine sadness at this outcome. I don't remember the burial.

These are such small fears, almost forgotten.

O ma mère (I cannot write this yet in English), if I were to let myself address you in these letters as I once did and hear no answer, my heart would impale itself on those tiny bat's claws.

June 9, 1993

noon

Dear Alice,

The bat is still there. I'm learning more about bats. They are nocturnal flying mammals with membranous wings who navigate by echolocation. Echolocation, I've discovered, is the emission of sound waves that return to the sender as echoes. A bat feeds on insects, nectar, fruit, flesh, or blood. Its face looks like a smudged dog. All this is fascinating to me, though I don't know why. You would be very surprised and pleased by my intense interest in such small forms of life.

I can't decide whether the baby bat is still waiting for the darkness that won't come. Even before the sun sets, the hall electric lights turn on automatically, so day and night would be indistinguishable to a mammal positioned as she is. I try to imagine always waiting for the dark, perhaps dying because it won't come. How tenaciously she clings to the rim of the window! Why doesn't she let go?

Or has rigor mortis immortalized her in that refusal to give up?

June 10, 1993
2 P.M.

Dear Alice,

Yesterday my letter to you was interrupted by the visit of a woman who had come to do Shiatsu acupressure therapeutic massage on my strained back. I really don't know what you would think of this. Lydia arrives with a fold-up table, a sheet, oils. There is no music, no chatting, no incense: just fingers finely reading every muscle and bone in my back. After the massage, she mentions that there is a bone in the human head shaped like a bat's wings.

I have learned that if you injure one part of your body, other parts change, realign themselves, twist, tighten, to compensate or protect. The woman giving the acupressure massage encourages me to trust myself more and always to listen to what my body is telling me. When I ask what stretching exercises to do, she says my body will know. I think you would have liked that. Maybe just that.

Today the bat seems to have collected small, sparkling white pieces of sand on its fur. I don't know why. Perhaps it was the severe thunderstorm yesterday afternoon. The day darkened and the radio told each nearby Connecticut town exactly when the "Storm Watch" would be over. In New Haven it was oddly specific: 4:45 P.M. I had been planning to buy onions I needed for dinner but fell asleep waiting for 4:45 P.M. I didn't even think to check on the bat.

Maybe that means I know she's dead.

There is no nectar, fruit, flesh, or blood to eat in that glassed-in space. Insects crawl near fearlessly. I don't think the sound waves she is capable of sending are returning as echoes.

These letters to you are my echolocations.

Dear Alice,

After all I've learned about the computer and its capacity for swallowing up and not regurgitating writing, I haven't "saved" these letters.

You were the one who believed, and convinced me, that if I could learn to type I could learn to use a computer.

After my first week of typing at the Marymount Graduate School Computer Center in Virginia, I lost the opening chapter of the book I was writing on directors in rehearsal. I drove back to your house with a deathly white face and told you. You were quiet and watched me. I sat on the couch next to your chair and tried to figure out what I had done wrong. (WordPerfect Customer Support couldn't explain it, though your eleven-year-old grandson, Robert, was willing to.) You listened and waited.

Finally, I said I would begin retyping the lost thirty pages the next day. With love you looked at me as if you'd been holding your breath. You said something about my climbing back on my horse. I noticed I was proud of myself.

I will "save" these letters to you, though ever since your death that word seems strange and impossible.

Dear Alice,

I have been reading some autobiographical reflections of William Trevor: "What children of a marriage rarely witness is the nature of the love that brought the whole thing—themselves included—into being in the first place. The marriage of parents is almost always mysterious: the sensual elements scarcely bear thinking about, the romantic past can only be guessed at, and all such curiosity invariably comes too late. What inadequately fills the vacuum now is sun-browned photographs of a young man in plus fours with hair brushed straight back. He stands by a motorcycle, and there's a misty image of the girl in the sidecar, her face mostly turned away." [1]

Today I came upon a "sun-browned" photograph of you and Dad, taken before your marriage, probably not long after you first met at Camp Mount Joy in New York. I had never seen it before.

My father is standing beside you in white slacks and shirt, his sleeves rolled up jauntily above jutting elbows, ends of fingers hooked into pants pockets, not a pose *I* ever saw. His left foot tilts gracefully at a diagonal, the toe just slightly raised. The pants look pressed, well-cut. His shirt is open at the collar; above is a young man's face, with a dimple in the left cheek. I see a smile of deep happiness and some pride on his face. His eyes are squinting a little, perhaps from too strong sunlight. He is very handsome.

To his right you stand.

You are wearing generously cut white shorts and a white blouse tucked in at the waist, with open collar and sleeves rolled up toward the shoulder, short white socks and white sports shoes with laces. The right leg receives most of the weight of your stance; the left leg is turned out slightly. Your black hair, windswept and shorter than I ever saw it, is falling just below the ear. Your indescribable eyes are far apart, dark, joyful. Your smile is a little wider and more open than my father's. There is a dimple on your right cheek. Your body is on a diagonal, your face tilted; your right arm hangs at your side, the left is hidden.

This is a picture of the love that "brought the whole thing . . . into being in the first place." I have seen all I can see.

And it is enough.

Camp Mount Joy, Alice Parson and Alfred Letzler.
New York, no date.

June 12, 1993
3:15 P.M.

Dear Alice,

Now I am looking at a photograph of you and me. The inscription in your handwriting says that I am four months old, so you must be twenty-eight. In the brown leather album you kept, you titled this photo, "Something To Be Proud Of." Now, I reverse your inscription: you are the something to be proud of.

I am just recognizably female, not quite bald, with startled eyebrows. The fingers of my right hand curve forward over your left shoulder as you hold me. My expression is serious but not grave. I stare at something beyond the frame of the picture. You are gazing at my face, your head tilted slightly back, to the right, to see your child and also to give the child her own space in the picture. Your left shoulder is raised a bit, pressed against your baby's body, giving support and comfort even as I rise above it, looking elsewhere.

You are wearing a cotton print dress, short-sleeved, with small ruffles on the sleeve. Your hair and brows are dark like your eyes. Your hair is now medium-length, pinned back simply behind the ear with a single bobby pin. One wisp trails down to the side of your left ear. You are smiling. The angle of your body gives a sense of graceful effortlessness, movement arrested in space.

I am held as much by your steady gaze as by your encircling arms. You embrace and secure an animated baby daughter without interfering with her exploratory glance and gesture.

Over half a century later, I look at myself being seen and not seeing. I involuntarily bend my head, trying to see into eyes shaded by their focus on me. I want so much to see you seeing me, to see you again, to see you as I never saw you. I crane my neck awkwardly. I want to get back into the photograph, to see the look that everyone present must have taken for granted and no one saw. There is no way to reenter the scene of the maternal gaze.

"Something To Be Proud Of," Susan and Alice Letzler.
Arlington, Virginia, October 1940.

June 12, 1993
6 P.M.

Dear Alice,

This is the day I must say goodbye to my friend Natalie who is moving to New Mexico. Sitting with her in front of a neighborhood pastry shop as she tries to give away four eight-week-old kittens, I notice growing in a nearby pot some delicate "money plants," the kind you used to cut in your backyard, dry in the basement, and carefully wrap for me to take back to my graduate student apartment in Cambridge. On the way home, the smells of hot dinners cooked near open windows, the child-size laundry drying on the line behind our apartment building, a single orange-and-yellow piece of candy corn lying on the sidewalk, and the final inning of a baseball game trumpeted from a radio somebody left on the grass remind me of long-ago Junes.

All the times I am not writing, unutterable letters beat in my heart.

June 13, 1993

10:15 P.M.

Dear Alice,

This was what you would call a real June day, and David and I spent most of it outdoors: eating, walking, sitting by water. It was as if a whole summer, unexpected and perfect, bloomed in one afternoon.

I remember a hot July evening in Virginia when you decided you were well enough to go to a nearby cluster of ethnic restaurants. We arrived just as they were all closing. I parked the car, left you there, and ran to buy dinner to bring home with us. Returning with no food and no ideas, I fell into a kind of void. You suggested that we keep driving and soon we came to a tiny take-out pizza place I hadn't been to since high school. I ordered, brought pizza and a large Pepsi back to the car. So we sat in the heat with the car doors open, eating from the cardboard box with our fingers, sharing our drink, and you suddenly looked across at me with your wonderful smile and said, "This is fun." And only now do I remember that I replied, *"You're fun."*

June 14, 1993
12:30 P.M.

Dear Alice,

Today on my way to have my hair cut I overheard a soft-voiced mother say to her young son, "I really don't know. You mean the only man *ever* in the *whole* world?"

If I asked questions that stumped you, I don't remember them. But then there were questions I never asked. I don't remember a conversation on sex and reproduction. I do remember several high school friends becoming pregnant before graduation.

One of my friends asked me to loan her ten dollars toward a wedding ring. Like me, she had been a class officer and an honors student; her pregnancy and quick marriage were a surprise. I asked you to loan me the money and explained why. I really didn't know what you'd say, especially since my friend hadn't confided in her own parents. Maybe I assumed you would refuse the money and then I wouldn't have to think about it anymore. But you took a stand, easily and calmly. As you handed me the ten dollars, you said that what mattered was not whether they had been married before the pregnancy but whether they loved one another. I don't know if that was your position in general or even in relation to your own children, but it gave me an entirely new sense of you.

I teach a college seminar on love poetry now. It assumes that the human experience of loving is no less complicated than the act of writing poetry, and that writing is itself a way of loving. As I write you, I wonder if this seminar had its impulse in your responding to a daughter's question about money with a mother's question about love.

June 15, 1993
2:30 P.M.

Dear Alice,

In this photograph I don't know you.

On the back, in a distant relative's hand, is written "Cousin Alice Parson." The long-ago photographer is S. Redfield, 112 East 125th Street, New York. Placed in front of what looks like a painted background of sky, trees, and hills, a tiny figure all in white stands on a raised platform near a table: rosebud lips, tousled short curly hair, calm penetrating gaze, head jauntily on a diagonal, left hand placed on the table top in an artificially crushed position, feet in white buttoned shoes at right angles, and, quite unexpectedly, a touch of petticoat showing.

This person I don't know is assuredly you.

All in White, Alice Parson.
New York City, no date.

Dear Alice,

For a long time after you died, the cry of Shakespeare's Lear mourning his dead daughter, Cordelia, would not go from my mind: "Why should a dog, a horse, a rat, have life, / And thou no breath at all?"[2]

I've always "had a problem" with death. Once when you visited us in New Haven, you had to convince me to throw out plants that had died weeks before your arrival.

Since last fall I have been carefully nurturing three African violets—one purple, one pink, and one blue. I remember the beautiful, endlessly blooming African violets on your kitchen windowsill. After you died, I gave them to one of your dearest friends, but they still flower in my mind.

These violets, my very first, were a gift from the president of my college in honor of the publication of the book whose first reader you were in the last year of your life. They sit side by side on my dining room windowsill, they have been watered together precisely as the directions indicate, they receive the same slant of sunlight. The pink one in the middle is dying; its few remaining leaves are yellow.

Sappho says:

> We know this much
>
> Death is an evil;
> we have the gods'
> word for it; they too
> would die if death
> were a good thing[3]

June 16, 1993
2:05 P.M.

Dear Alice,

Watching you make a new address book after Dad died, I thought I'd never have the patience.

One day last December, my twenty-five-year-old address book broke in two as I was writing Christmas and Hanukkah cards. So, before I sent out invitations in January to my and David's joint book-signing party in New York, I made a new address book. I thought of you, patient and uncomplaining, as I labored, transferring entries, omitting names of persons no longer alive or whose current whereabouts were unknown. There were so many.

When I came to the L's, I copied your name, the address of the house that other people own, and the phone number that I called every night for eight years after Dad's death until you couldn't speak any more.

I was radiantly happy at the book party and I missed you beyond measure. Three summers ago, a week before you died, you finished proofreading my first typed draft. You were ready now, you said, to read the galleys.

June 16, 1993
2:55 P.M.

Dear Alice,

Looking back through my "broken" address book, I see faded names of people I barely remember: Tip Ruangchotvit (filed under "T," apparently because I couldn't be counted on to remember his last name), Economist, Land Policy Division, Land Development Dept., Ministry of Nat'l. Dev., Bangkok, Thailand. "Tip," of course, wouldn't have been his real name. I don't really remember "Tip," but he was one of a stream of people who were overnight guests in your house as the years went by.

You never said no; if there wasn't an available bed, there was the living room couch. Relatives, of course, but also your children's friends from high school, college, graduate school, and beyond would camp out there. You remember how my high school friend Chip slept on a foldaway bed in our basement, with private entrance and bathroom, one summer while his parents were in Alaska? Friends of friends, visiting Washington or traveling north or south, would stay over and tenors performing in productions of the Northern Virginia Opera boarded free for many seasons.

In the last few years of your life, your own friends would come, one at a time. They would stay longer than the other guests had, and in between their visits I would reclaim my bedroom. In the fall of 1989, a German graduate student researching her dissertation lived in your house as a boarder for seven weeks; Claudia returned as a friend in the spring and stayed with you four months, almost until the end of your life.

Just before you died, I arranged for a full-time companion who would sleep upstairs in your bedroom.

That was the only time you ever resisted.

June 17, 1993
5:30 P.M.

Dear Alice,

The "oral history" tapes you made at my request the autumn before you died—I haven't been able to listen to them for almost three years. I don't even know why. It's just our voices talking, isn't it?

June 18, 1993

11 A.M.

Dear Alice,

You were always happy working on a project or helping someone, and you made sure you had plenty of opportunities: you found
affordable housing for public school teachers moving to Arlington,
coedited the Arlington Forest newspaper with Dad, taught homebound children and children for whom English was a second language, arranged and publicized events for the Performing Arts
Division of the Arlington County Recreation Department, helped
create a lip-reading program for Washington Public Television,
served on the Northern Virginia Opera Board for thirty years,
co-coordinated the impressive multinational Northern Virginia
Folk Festival for over a decade.

You seemed to cherish all these projects that took you outside
your family role and, at the same time, motherhood. My brother and
I felt equally loved as your children. Or—the greater miracle—we
each probably thought ourselves the more completely loved. After I
entered college, I often asked what you would change in your life, if
you could, and you always replied, "Nothing." At first, I was openly
disbelieving, then, later, awed.

I stopped asking after Dad died.

Dear Alice,

There are so many taken-for-granted events in your life that I turn over now in my mind. When you picked a single rose from your garden, or in later years asked me to, and placed it in a tiny cut-glass rose vase for us to smell and see, or bent over your purple African violets to water them after cooking dinner, or asked me when I visited if I had noticed the crape myrtle blooming after so many barren seasons, why did it never occur to me to wonder what undertow quietly washed through you?

Now, like you, I look for changes in the moon each night; I actually notice the smell of summer-bleached grass and the tentative colors of spring flowers just budding. I am beginning to read the "little books" you always kept near you: the one on garden flowers, "illustrated in color," and the one called *Talking Leaves,* and Roger Tory Peterson's field guide to the birds you loved to watch for.

I never knew how I would miss Virginia and your house in summer: the thunderous chatter of small birds outside the upstairs bedroom windows before dawn, the melancholy sound of two turtle doves who lived just over the back fence, the wily black squirrel you could never trick out of overturning the new glass bird feeder before the robins and cardinals and blue jays and sparrows could arrive. Once as night fell, you and I sat on your front steps listening to the astonishing repertoire of a mockingbird high up on a telephone pole.

When Claudia came back from Cologne to stay with you, she kept a methodical schedule. Every evening after supper she would sit for half an hour on your back porch watching the lit sky. The few times I sat with her the sky seemed so ordinary to me. How extraordinarily painful it is to remember that now.

June 21, 1993

10 P.M.

Dear Alice,

Tonight I ironed a pair of men's pajamas for the first time. It is harder than I expected; parts around the seat are not accessible to first-time pajama ironers and creases ironed out on one side of a sleeve reproduce themselves inversely on the other side. Looking up the word "inversely," out of idle curiosity, I notice a tiny sketch on the right side of the entry for "intestine" in *Webster's New World Dictionary,* and there I see all those organs so close together—stomach, pancreas, colon, and liver—that, cancerous, took the lives of Dad, his sister, your mother, you.

It was you who first bought David the only kind of pajamas he wears—long-sleeved, drawstring, solid-color cotton—and you seemed to think I would iron them, even mentioned it once casually. I responded with vehemence: women of my generation don't iron their husbands' pajamas! You were slightly taken aback, I think, more baffled than shocked. You never brought it up again and continued to buy him pajamas. You would not intrude in matters that had to do with my married life. I think it was as much a mystery to you as yours was to me.

I ironed these pajamas because I am sending them to your grandson, Ben. I bought David the same size you always bought, but they don't fit. Somehow I'm not surprised.

June 22, 1993
9:55 P.M.

Dear Alice,

Goethe says, "Don't look for anything behind the phenomena; they themselves are the theory."[4]

My pink African violet now seems to be flowering and dying at the same time.

June 25, 1993
11:45 A.M.

Dear Alice,

I've been thinking a lot about vacations lately, wondering if there's a trick to them that I've forgotten.

You resisted the *idea* of vacations. You marveled once that you never wore out Dad's patience or his stamina in resisting your resistance. Once launched, however, you were the cheerful, non-grumpy vacationer in the family. As an adolescent, I refused to share your delight in each new site we visited in our summer drives south or west. Poor Dad: resistances on every side, yet he persisted.

Dad really loved to plan trips. He was careful and intelligent and orderly in most things, including his own dying. Truly astounding were his great gifts as a packer. For my first trip to Europe with two friends, he suggested that I pack my suitcases in layers whose contents were determined by the anticipated frequency of use of each article. We made a diagram of this system on 3x5 cards. For eight weeks I impressed my friends and myself, magically finding whatever I needed as we traveled rapidly from city to city and country to country.

After Dad died, I tried to continue his system. Perhaps packing was the key to success.

The first trip you and I took by ourselves was a few months after your cancer operation. You wanted a vacation badly. You had already begun to call this your "lost summer." But I didn't have Dad's experience in knowing how to proceed. Without making hotel reservations, we began to pack for a three-day trip to The Homestead, an elegant resort in southwestern Virginia. For days we selected outfits and bathing suits and jewelry. You remember how Ken came to your house the night before we were to leave and loaded the car (we had more luggage than I'd taken to Europe). Early the next morning there were reports of a hurricane hurtling through Virginia. The rain had already begun to fall heavily. I looked at you and you asked what we should do. Without hesitation, I said, "We've packed our ear-rings. We have to go."

I searched your eyes for resistance and, with wonder, saw none. And that was a trip we never stopped talking about.

June 26, 1993
1:45 P.M.

Dear Alice,

Today Ken, Joyce, and your two grandsons are traveling by train from Washington, D.C., to New Haven. My brother suggested that I check the time of their arrival, reminding me of the six-hour delay of an ill-fated Amtrak train you and I once took to Washington: the Yankee Clipper finally arrived at midnight, surviving *two* malfunctioning engines, a fire just north of New York City, and tracks buckling from extreme heat, which brought it to a standstill at Philadelphia.

I had boarded the Yankee Clipper in New Haven and you were to board it at a prearranged time in New York after visiting your friend Bea Taruskin in Brooklyn. You had been waiting for several hours at Penn Station when there was a booming announcement: "The Yankee Clipper has been sighted." Such an announcement, you told me later, almost made the wait bearable. Once you entered the train, we had to find each other quickly. You remained stationary and I walked through car after car. Suddenly I saw your glorious smile. Your friend Florence's husband, Elliott Shapiro, who had sat with you in the station all those hours, quietly slipped away. We found seats together, and during the next train crisis at Philadelphia happily shared the few provisions I had brought—small cans of tomato juice, crackers, Vermont cheddar cheese, grapes, and two peaches.

We talked nonstop.

As night fell, the passengers in our car began to share stories, food, newspapers. Someone may have had a radio.

By the time we arrived in the nation's capital at midnight, the whole experience, like the evening air, had about it something unreal. Ken was waiting to drive us to your house, where we discovered he had already brought fresh milk and turned on the air conditioning. I noticed that his thoughtfulness did not surprise you: he was your son.

My brother and I have largely lost the self-identifying words, "son" and "daughter," just as, except with him, I have lost the word (I force myself to write this), "Mom." Now my brother makes his first visit to me. How happy it would make you to see me meet *him* at the station.

June 27, 1993

noon

Dear Alice,

Two days ago our downstairs neighbor discovered the baby bat. A scientist, she declared it dead and starting to decompose. The next day it was gone. I feel oddly bereft.

I had been looking at the bat almost every day, and I never noticed any decomposing. I only saw its tightened claws clinging to the rim of the window, "holding on for dear life" (a cliché you resuscitated for me).

All that's left of her is what I've written.

June 27, 1993
11 P.M.

Dear Alice,

I once taught myself to sketch in order to see. I sketched many things: stubby chimney tops in London, Connecticut trees in light wind, David reading in bed, small figurines, my own hand. Now I write in order to remember.

I remember your grandson Robert's first "story." Ken's family and you and Dad and I were vacationing in Sandbridge Beach, Virginia, and one night I asked Robert, who was very young, to make up a story. When he was silent, I asked him several specific questions about possible characters and plot, and his answers produced a story that I wrote down for him. It featured a family in which everyone including the dog had the same name: Danziger. That's all I can remember except that you saved it.

my wedding anniversary
June 28, 1993
12:30 P.M.

Dear Alice,

Near the end of your life you tentatively suggested that I might write your "story." I am struck by your trust, and your inviting a kind of writing that surprises me every day. The story I learn to tell is the story of failing to tell your "story."

David just came in and surprised me with pink roses on our anniversary. This letter must end now.

Dear Alice,

When I think of you, I think of intelligence encircled by kindness.

July 1, 1993
4:30 P.M.

Dear Alice,

During the last eight years of your life, when we performed our "telephone ritual" of talking just before you fell asleep, I remember thinking we ought to vary the hour at which we spoke so that I would not fixate on it after your death. How simple my notion of mourning was.

I still have not lost the habit of storing up random details from the day to share with you.

David and I are in Manhattan. At 5 A.M. I awaken in the sweltering city heat, look out the window, and see that the flower shop across the street has a new feature: a television. The flower shop originated as a twenty-four-hour, open-air site on the sidewalk, protected only by the awning of a delicatessen nearby. Business improved. Heavy plastic covering shielded purchasers from disagreeable weather. Later, glass-and-wood walls and a door appeared. Eventually there were signs of electricity, and now the television. Though these improvements should make it impossible, I smell the flowers from my fourth-floor window.

You always noticed, and loved, growing things. There were no cut flowers at your funeral and none on your grave.

I don't think you would like the view from this window.

July 1, 1993
11:45 P.M.

Dear Alice,

A line from Keats catches my eye: "They seek no wonder but the human face."[5]

Now I remember the last time we each saw the other's human face. As I watched you nap, two lines of Wordsworth came into my mind. When you awakened, and asked me what I was thinking, I quoted them: "To me the meanest flower that blows can give / Thoughts that do often lie too deep for tears."[6] I remember you found interesting my suggestion that these lines might be connected to Virgil's "sunt lacrimae rerum"[7] ("these are the tears of things"), and so together we looked up the Latin words in your old Latin dictionary. I left you that afternoon; when I returned to Virginia three days later, you were in a coma, in what the nurse called "an inappropriate sleep" that lasted just as long as the oncologist said it would.

I didn't cry when I quoted Wordsworth's lines; now, when I read them aloud in class, thoughts of you lie too deep for tears.

I am humbled by my own lingering question, unanswerable and barely askable: how can anyone die in the midst of undying love?

July 2, 1993
noon

Dear Alice,

Today I polished your beautiful silver coffee pot, the one with the initials AL, until I could see a human face reflected in it. I don't know why I did that. I never use it, and anyway, it wasn't the right face.

Dear Alice,

Summers in New England: layers and layers of clothing are re-moved. Men take on the shape of pregnant women: sturdy legs under swollen bellies.

I imagine the zigzagging conversation this silly observation would have left in its wake.

July 2, 1993
11:30 P.M.

Dear Alice,

Searching through my old Sierra Club calendar for something else, I find on one date a single entry: "Mom—nightmares."

How terrifying to be alone with your nightmares!

And how appalling to find a phrasing so condensed that its author cannot decode it. I feel doubly lost reading it.

But you, what did you feel that night?

July 3, 1993
1 P.M. and 10 P.M.

Dear Alice,

I awakened this morning thinking of pills, and how you hated taking any, even aspirin, and one pill I never told you I was taking when you were dying, and trying to figure out why.

Your medication piled up: pills for infection, pills for pain, pills for nausea induced by chemotherapy, pills for depression induced first by the disease and then by its treatment, pills to counteract the effects of other pills. It got so complicated that I made two charts, one organized by days of the week and the other by the names and dosages of the pills themselves. Even with both charts, it was a maze that had to be re-explained to anyone trying to keep track when I was not there. And yet despite your hatred of all these pills, you yourself kept this schedule in mind and would help us remember when we were overwhelmed.

Some of the pills were so big that we bought a blue plastic pill splitter, and I remember how you watched from your chair as I sat at the card table and taught myself to divide pills evenly with "only the light pressure of a single finger." Too much pressure and the pill splintered into dustlike fragments.

Weeks before and for two weeks after your death, I took a pill on my own irregular schedule, a light tranquilizer that I had asked my doctor to prescribe after your cancer was confirmed. Why was it so hard to tell you this?

We talked about far harder things: we sat side by side in your doctor's office and heard your diagnosis; together we listened to the words of surgeons, oncologists, nurses, social workers; you yourself asked for your prognosis, and, finally, when you were ready, you asked me how you would die. I told you what the Boston oncologist I called had told me. Patients with liver cancer, he said, died a "compassionate death" (a phrase almost as shocking then as it is now): a slowing down of body functions, sleepiness during the day, listlessness, a profound lassitude followed by a coma lasting no longer than five days, then death. He didn't prepare me for the writhing, the administering of morphine to a woman who had natural childbirth without an aspirin, the difficult breathing, the undercurrent of speechless communication in a handclasp's slightest change of pressure.

I guess I didn't tell you about my pill because at first I didn't want you to think you were worse off than you were; then, when there was no worse, because I didn't want you to think you were overburdening my ability to take care of you; finally, perhaps, because I felt your admiration for whatever composure I managed to bring to moments that were increasingly heartbreaking.

Maybe I could have been what I was without this secret ally; maybe you wouldn't have cared a bit about it; maybe you might have felt joined somehow or even relieved. I'll never know.

But I needed to tell you this and no time was ever the right time. Until now.

July 3, 1993
11:15 P.M.
July 4, 1993
4 A.M.

Dear Alice,

Tonight is the full moon. It is so beautiful, with small irregular black patches suddenly veiling it and then departing. One part of the sky is lit by flashes of light accompanied by the sounds of early firecrackers. The scent of honeysuckle is especially strong tonight, like the honeysuckle near your house. These sounds, that smell, like the cries of mourning doves I hear every morning, recall a lost time and place.

At 4 A.M. the moon is brilliant; it floods the living room. Did you watch it at this hour?

Dear Alice,

How you loved the fireworks on the Fourth of July, the Arlington ones live and Washington's bigger show on television. I dimly
recall accompanying you, unwillingly, to parades in Colonial dress
near our little neighborhood library. Even the summer after Dad
died on the last day of June, the family still went to see the fireworks.
By then I didn't care so much about what we saw as what you were
teaching me by going.

We did nothing particularly patriotic today, although David listened to the staff of NPR read aloud the Declaration of Independ-
ence on the radio this morning. But in the evening we went out to
have supper by the beach, hot dogs and hamburgers and buttered
corn on the cob, and then we walked down close to the water to
watch seagulls and children enjoy the low tide. When we returned
to our apartment building, a very small child in white underpants
was striding through a two-foot plastic wading pool waving a tiny
American flag.

Right now I am looking at a wrinkled orange-and-yellow paper
bag in which I have kept six nondescript shells and a wisp of what
looks like dried seaweed from a summer day in Virginia at Sandbridge Beach when you and Dad were both well. I have a color
photo of you and me on that beach, tan and happy in our bathing
suits, our arms thrown around each other's waists. I don't know of
another photo of us like it, so carefree and caught in the moment.

But there was an unphotographed moment I cherish more. It
was at the end of a day in Sandbridge when adults and young children had conflicting plans and no plans had included simply sitting
on the sand or swimming in the ocean. After dinner, feeling a little
melancholy, I walked onto the beach and saw the rectangular rubber
float I had given my brother as a present. The sea at that hour was ir-
resistible. I waded in, jumped on the float, and then lay motionless
on the moving water, happy simply to be somewhere between sky

By the Sea, Alice Parson Letzler and Susan Letzler Cole.
Sandbridge Beach, Virginia, August 1981.

and sea. I didn't notice it was getting dark until I had floated beyond any site I could recognize. I began to paddle a little uncertainly against a stronger current than I had remembered, looking toward the beach for something familiar. Then I saw you sitting there, un-obtrusively, at my point of origin. You must have followed me out, understanding, even sharing, my impulse. You became the site I fo-cused on, and I paddled until the float bumped down in front of you.

You did not mention my leaving the beach house so abruptly. You were simply taking pleasure in my new happiness and we sat to-gether, talking quietly on the beach, watching the clumps of people who had now gathered by the water to fish and to cook what they caught, and maybe I collected these forgotten shells and the wisp of seaweed then.

As it grew darker, Ken and Joyce and Robert and Ben and Dad wandered out looking for us and again there were no questions, just a joining in the pleasure of an unplanned scene, the surrender to what we had come to do.

It helps now to remember that you were there even when I didn't know it. That is the power of the maternal gaze: we act as if it is not there, all the while hoping that it is.

July 5, 1993
1:15 P.M.

Dear Alice,

For the first year after you died I was not able to hold images of your dying in my mind for more than a few seconds at a time. My respiratory system would accelerate and then jam. At the same time, in my dreams you would become younger and younger, healthy and even more vibrant. Your hair was black again and you had no cane. In one startling dream you had remarried a somewhat younger, stocky man who spoke Spanish, a language neither of us ever knew. And you had a new baby. I remember in my dream being filled with delight and wonder, and then more wonder at my lack of jealousy. I had always been curious about what it would be like to have a sister, and now you had returned and brought forth other offspring, including my joy that remained long after the dream ended.

But there were sisters you gave me during your life. One of Claudia's beautiful, loving letters arrived today from Cologne. Her English is so elegant now that I can barely believe it is not her first language. I remember her arrival from what was then West Germany and how we talked as much with our faces and gestures and shy smiles as with words. And I remember how as the weeks passed the German dictionary seemed to be a little more remotely placed in the room and how both of you picked up the slang of the other's native language. Sometimes I felt as if I were the alien, as you and Claudia sat studying one after another American custom that I was in the habit of passing up: the Miss America contest, detective shows on television, and certain sitcoms. (These were at first difficult for Claudia, but after several months she began to laugh *before* you did.) All those parts of American history and culture she was as hungry for as you were for life.

At my suggestion Claudia organized your evening walks and joined you in a last look at the moon. And you entered into the crises of her own life with all the energy of a new mother.

And your dear Bev, once my student, after her return from Nigeria took you to her heart the instant she first greeted you at your door with chrysanthemums, saying, "Mums for the Mum." Little did she know. You became her "Virginia Mom" and then, after the birth of Thomas, her "Virginia Grandma," and I don't believe there was any crucial life-matter she didn't discuss with you except that she feared she was going to move away before you died. But you didn't let that happen.

I remember Bev telling me that once after she called to chat with you and got no answer, she put her training for the marathon to use running the two miles between her house and yours. When she arrived in record time, you were standing by your roses in the back yard, smiling.

Now Bev writes to tell me she has a new baby girl: "Sarah is lovely, your Mom would be smitten."[8] And she also has a new teaching position at a midwestern university, in the African and African American studies program. She doesn't say but I know we are both thinking how proud you would have been.

Bev mentions you in every letter, and she doesn't always write in the past tense: "It was your Mom's birthday last month and I thought of her fondly. A while ago Tom fell head-first into the creek (over the bridge) which is lined with jagged boulders and concrete blocks at the edge. He sustained *not a scratch*. It's at times like those that I know your Mom is watching over him. He's lucky to have such a guardian angel." Angels are very fashionable now, but I don't think Bev is responding to a fashion.

And, finally, there is Barbara, a former coordinator of the Northern Virginia Folk Festival who became an actress and part-time teacher in New York. Barbara's furniture remained in your basement for four years, a situation you always defended as appropriate to her needs despite complaints by those who knew how deeply you cared for the absence of clutter. Only at the end of this arrangement did I understand that Barbara herself inhabited a part of that house through her constant devotion to you. She listened, she took and gave counsel, she sent souvenirs, she called and wrote, she remembered the important dates of your life, and she was the only one brave enough to call me on the first anniversary of your death. She wrote me recently that what she had from you that meant more than anything else was a sense of unconditional love. And I know what she means, because I had it too.

Barbara came to David's and my book party in New York this January. I hadn't seen her in many years, and she had changed the style and color of her hair. For quite a while I felt a warm and steady gaze coming at me from a few feet away. Finally, Barbara moved closer and said, "I've been watching your smile; it reminds me of Alice."

And I think that was the first time I understood how your daughters need each other, all of us, the one you gave birth to and the ones who arrive by other means, even the ones I dream for you.

Dear Alice,

I think about how you loved the mountains, and never lived there.

Your two brothers, both doctors, did: Bill in the hills near Charlottesville and Rudy near a small mountain, half of which he owned, in Logantown, Pennsylvania. Uncle Bill was a "gentleman farmer," with a few cows and horses and mainly a lot of chickens and woods. But Uncle Rudy had a real dairy farm with a name, "Rudson Farm." I remember once, as a child at Rudson Farm, your allowing me to be hoisted onto a large tractor that I "drove," seated in front of a much larger, older cousin, and I remember feeding the cows and being shown the salt lick for deer (which I didn't quite understand) halfway up the mountain. What intrigued me most, though, was indoors: strips of "fly paper" that hung from the ceiling of the porch off the living room and mysteriously attracted the hordes of farm flies that liked to accompany every activity. I don't remember what you did at Rudson Farm that made you so happy, just that you always were. It was being with your beloved older brother, of course, but it was also the mountains.

The last time we went to Rudy's farm was for his funeral, and that's when we heard everyone refer to him as "Doctor." I guess for me his being a doctor wasn't as real as his being a large, red-haired, good-natured farming man. And when I think about it, you must have felt the same way.

Your antipathy toward doctors and hospitals was famous for as long as I knew you: you could have lived your whole life without ever visiting any doctor except your two brothers.

Rudson Farm, I discover, has disappeared from your new address book without a trace. Uncle Bill's address in Charlottesville has also vanished. He moved on to other locations, first in the hills of Berkeley, California, and then in a house designed by Aunt Buffy and constructed on a remote plot of land in the mountains far north of San

Francisco and never visited by you or me. Now I enter Bill and Buffy's new Seattle address in your book.

Bill is not a practicing physician. He and Rudy seem different in every way except in their devotion to you. Rudy was a country doctor, a farmer, father of two sons and a daughter, a convert to Catholicism sometime before his death (a fact you discovered at his burial when he was placed beside his wife). Bill is a cultured academic doctor and former chairman of the department of internal medicine at the University of Virginia for seventeen years, where he still teaches a course each fall when he is not training residents at Makerere University in Kampala, Uganda; he is the father of four sons; his religion is undiscussed.

Our visits to Rudy's farm were irregular, but the visits to Bill's farm were not. Every Christmas and every Fourth of July, we drove to Charlottesville with presents or watermelon. It was so much a part of our lives that it feels funny now to see it as a tradition actually established by someone. But it must have been, and my guess is that you and Buffy created it. However it was decided, it was never questioned in our family, nor was our spending every Thanksgiving with Dad's family in New York City. The "New York Thanksgiving" survived the deaths of those who presided over it, my grandparents, and many of those who enjoyed it most: my father, his sister Anne, and his brother Eddie who always brought jars of those extraordinary pickles, fresh from the Lower East Side, that Dad took home with us to savor for months afterward, like vintage wines.

I thought after Dad died you might give up the frenetic drive north the day before Thanksgiving, but for a few years more you came, and even after you stopped, you encouraged me to keep coming. Until then I never thought I believed in family traditions.

I wonder if you anticipated the consequences of the rituals you staged in your and your children's lives. Did you calculate, or just hope for, certain outcomes? Did you and Dad simply live in a way that seemed to make sense, day by day, season by season, opportunity by opportunity, hoping for happiness and, in the end, accepting life's nonnegotiable terms?

I wonder, too, if you had been Rudy and Bill's *brother,* would you, like them, have lived high in the hills, by the mountains that gave you such joy? But how can I imagine another life for you without reimagining my own?

July 5, 1993
9 P.M.

Dear Alice,

A friend gave me a novel that she said I would need to know the end of *Tosca* to appreciate. Tonight I looked for your little book of opera summaries, but I cannot find it.

I remember so clearly the afternoon you were asked to substitute for someone who was to have spoken on a Verdi opera that evening at the main public library in Arlington. You compiled notes on 3x5 cards, identified musical passages to be played during your talk, rehearsed a few times with me (I was to work the record player), all with the kind of composure I still only dream of. We heard a knock at the door and there was Chip, a college professor turned independent farmer, unexpectedly standing on the front steps holding a carton of farm-fresh eggs. Without a look at the clock, you invited him in and he sat while we scrambled, ate, and complimented the eggs. Then, with fifteen minutes to spare, you dressed, I drove you to the library, and for the first time in my life I heard you "teach" a work of art.

Your public voice was different from the "home" voice I knew. It seemed deeper, sharper, more formally attentive to the articulation of every syllable, yet still as musical and engaging as the voice that had read bedtime stories in my childhood. I don't know if you saw the shining in my eyes or could accept my singing your praises afterwards, but even today I can see you taking command of the moment and loving it.

Dear Alice,

Mothers are omnipresent on Connecticut beaches this summer. When you returned from vacations with my brother and his family, you told me that in Delaware everybody brought a grandmother to the beach. But here, today, at Hammonassett, it is mothers' voices I hear everywhere. "Benjamin, get off the blanket, we're leaving." "I don't know, Sarah. Where did you lose it?" "Your head, under. Danny, slow stroke." "That's what happens at the beach, Mikey. Your pants are *supposed* to get dirty and wet. It's all right. No, I didn't bring your other trunks." "Mikey, put your pants back on."

It's hard sometimes to imagine why mothers are so happy at the beach, but it's a place I remember as full of delight for a child. When I was three and wandered off on my own at Jones Beach, if it was traumatic to you I never knew it. Chatting under a lifeguard's hat when you collected me at the Lost and Found, I never conceived of myself as lost. Not then, certainly.

Hammonassett is a beach I think you would love. A narrow boardwalk separates high grass and dunes from a long, wide expanse of white sand dotted with mostly families. There are brightly colored beach umbrellas in many styles; some little tents for babies; beach chairs just like yours that sink into the sand; coolers for soft drinks, juice, fruit; a little boy digging furiously with a large yellow shovel, until he disappears into his hole. Four African American preadolescents, two girls and two boys, play shoulder-deep in the water for hours, then emerge, fully dressed; two older couples walk past on the boardwalk speaking rapid vigorous Russian; seagulls, not in their usual line, are sprinkled around us like sentinels guarding a blanket-size settlement. A grandmother carefully washes all parts of a naked child (Mikey) in the ocean and then carries him across the sand to deposit him shining and clean in his mother's lap.

If you could sit with me on the beach now and see what I see, would you enjoy it more than when we were young? Or less?

Dear Alice,

I remember the last vacation you and I took. It was mid-July, 1989. We stayed in a small hotel in Tidewater Virginia. The second night there, you ate many courses at dinner, most of them to do with fish. You looked very pretty in your white suit and light pink blouse. After dinner when we returned to our room, you said, very calmly and quietly, that you didn't want to alarm me but you thought you might be sick from all that seafood. You went into the bathroom, re-moved your suit jacket and blouse, then came out and lay down on the bed. All you asked was that I adjust the temperature control to cool the room. This kind of adjustment had first been performed by a young man who had brought our luggage to the room, and I hadn't watched. I had been more concerned with the view from our window.

That was all you asked of me. I was reaching toward the temper-ature control above your bed when I looked down at your face, white, distressed, helpless. I made a sudden instinctive adjustment and the room cooled; you were able to get ready for bed, the unex-pected nausea seemed to lessen, and you fell asleep. I lay awake in my bed until 4 A.M., listening to the soft Southern voice of a local woman deejay who talked me through the night.

Before I fell asleep, I looked again at the view. The river widened to the shape of a lake in front of the hotel. And under a full moon, I saw someone on the far shore stepping into a small boat. A lamp il-luminated the path of the slowly moving vessel until it reached the exact middle of the river where for a long time I watched a solitary figure patiently fishing by the light of the moon.

I wanted to share this when you awakened, but we had so much to do. The next morning, at home, your surgeon telephoned and scheduled the CAT scan that in two weeks would reveal what he called "a spot on the liver."

Dear Alice,

Right now I'm on hold for WordPerfect Customer Support. So many times, in your house, I would sit talking to you in just this situation.

A man with a slight Southwestern accent listens to my problem: every time I attempt to enter this writing where I left off (by pressing "Home" twice and the "down" arrow once), the computer takes me to a blank screen always exactly twenty pages ahead of my last letter to you. I seem forever unable to catch up with the end of my own writing.

The slow-speaking voice tells me I have a "corrupt file" and proposes an elaborate scenario that involves removing all the codes for the file and replacing them. Without knowing much about computers, you can imagine why that might not seem the ideal remedy. So I continue to describe my problem. Finally, he thinks of a very simple solution, which I effect in a couple of seconds.

In the Museum of Natural History one summer in New York, David and I saw Tibetan monks constructing a mandala in sand. They work slowly over several months, and when they are through, they wipe it away at a stroke. Until this moment I thought I might be content to do the same thing.

July 9, 1993
midnight and noon

Dear Alice,

May I retell the "red wagon story"? I always said I had forgiven you long ago, but you were never quite sure.

Here it is for the last time, an episode we both wished to forget and never got around to burying. This is the burial.

The mother of my friend Joey, whose father was killed in World War II, had borrowed your Underwood typewriter (the one you kept, cherished, and used for the rest of your life). Joey's mother didn't have a typewriter, probably didn't have money to buy one, needed to type something important. When she was ready to return your Underwood, you sent me with my red wagon to pick it up. On the way back, Joey, pulling the wagon along the sidewalk with me inside holding the typewriter, had to negotiate a slope and a corner. Excited, Joey began to speed up; I grabbed the sides of the wagon. As we shot around the corner, the wagon veered wildly and turned over. I was unharmed, but the Underwood spilled onto the pavement. We put it back in the wagon, there at the corner, halfway between our two apartments. I remember thinking that since Joey was the one who had tipped over the wagon, we should go back to *his* mother and have her fix it. But we went on, delivering a broken typewriter to you. In front of Joey you said you were sorry for what happened and you would pay for the damage.

My eight-year-old's sense of justice was outraged.

This was not the first time. On the opening day of kindergarten, my friend Ronnie had whispered to me while we were supposed to be quiet. The teacher, who heard one voice but saw two heads together, told both of us to stand in the corner (separate corners). When I came home that day, I announced that I was not going back to kindergarten: it was an institution that promoted injustice. And you supported me.

Two little chapters in my early life, and I never connected them. If I had, I would have understood your response to the Kindergarten

Crisis as that of someone who cared for justice—but what exactly would have been a "just" ending to the red wagon story?

Retelling this removes the codes of a "corrupt file." There was nothing to forgive.

I have already forgiven the only unforgivable act of your life, one you resisted with all your being. For an hour after the doctor pronounced you dead, you held my cold hand, warming it with yours.

Dear Alice,

At your funeral I saw Ben remove his dark bow tie and drop it on your casket. Later he told me he had first considered placing a lock of his hair in your coffin. It had never occurred to me to do such a thing. I was still waiting to learn how much of me had not gone with you into your grave.

The television has announced that a "dangerous" thunderstorm is approaching. It is almost too hot to write you. We have had five days of stifling humidity and temperatures above 90 degrees and are promised at least five more. I remember worrying during the week in the summer when Aunt Anne was staying with you. You told me you only left the house to turn on the sprinkler in the backyard at the times designated for outdoor watering. But you survived the heat and the enforced proximity.

I remember the bitter cold night when the furnace broke after you went to bed and I silently covered you with as many blankets as I could find while you slept.

The rain is falling steadily.

These seasonal changes, these extremes of hot and cold, are sensations I wish for you now.

Dear Alice,

At the end of my first year at college, while Dad drove us home, I talked to you nonstop for five hours. I don't remember a single thing I said. I never forgot the experience of being listened to that way.

I didn't, then, know that truly paying attention to someone else is the rarest kind of human love.

July 12, 1993
8 A.M. and 10 P.M.

Dear Alice,

Forgotten events in my life come back in dreams. When I awake, I have the lost event and the dream, each calling to the other.

I dreamed of you again last night. Always in dreams of the dead there is something that indicates absence, that acknowledges the reality of loss. I used to dream of Dad after his death: he was there, but he couldn't speak or else he wasn't wearing his proper clothes. For a long time I dreamed of you young, vibrant, active; then, after a while, hints of physical weakness appeared. Last night's dream was a surprise. It reawakened a memory of the evening—it was one of my last visits to you—when my wallet was stolen on my arrival at the Washington train station. You had to pay my cab fare to Arlington; I didn't have a dime as I entered your house. The absence of all my usual forms of identification was more upsetting to me than the loss of money, which you immediately replaced. Despite your illness, you went with me to obtain one piece of personal identification, then proposed lunch, which you were almost able to finish, at a restaurant overlooking the Potomac. You took the trauma out of this theft. Last night brought the trauma back, but it was you who were stolen.

In my dream, David and I were riding the New York subway that somehow took us to your house in Northern Virginia. As we emerged from the subway car, my pocketbook seemed almost weightless. I opened it and found it was empty. At your house I itended to call the police to report a theft but couldn't find the number. Standing by the phone in your upstairs bedroom, I noticed two radios side by side on a small table. One was mine, a gift from you and Dad when I had measles as a child; music was playing and I couldn't make it stop without unplugging the radio. Suddenly there was a pungent smell of ironing in the air. A woman, not you, appeared, ironing. No one but you had ever ironed in that room.

Finally, in the most banal way possible, I had dreamed your death, and just before I awakened I thought, I must write her about it tonight.

July 13, 1993
1:30 P.M.

Dear Alice,

You appeared last night as vividly as you ever had.

In this dream, I had come alone to visit you and Dad in Virginia, but was leaving to meet a friend. You asked, in a half-joking way, when we immortals would next meet. I said, quite seriously, "Whenever you want, we can meet again."

You seemed relieved by that reply and, sensing something unspoken, I asked whether you wanted to talk to me now. You smiled and said, "Yes," almost shyly. Overwhelmed, I hugged you hard, but suddenly you had no body weight and I awoke. David was at my side, his hand still holding mine with the slight pressure of one fast asleep. I lay in darkness, my vision of luminous presence ungraspable.

July 14, 1993
12 A.M.

Dear Alice,

    We have not ended our conversations. How could we? I am still learning what we were saying.

Dear Alice,

David and I are watching a series of films about the peoples and cultures of Africa. Organized by the African Studies Outreach Program at Yale, it was advertised as open to the public. The most deeply affecting film was *Camp de Thiaroye,* by Ousmane Sembène and Thierno Faty Sow. This time I stayed afterward for the discussion.

In *Camp de Thiaroye,* a man returns to his village after fighting for the French in World War II. He asks where his family is, and two relatives turn their backs in silence. He will learn that his father and mother have been killed by soldiers. An African filmmaker in the audience explained that a death could not be announced immediately: first, there must be drinking of water and the formal statement that all is well. He added that there is no word for "death" in Wolof, the African language spoken in the film.

When the death to be announced is your own, what is the protocol? I remember Dad's face the day after his surgeon told him that his cancer was inoperable, terminal. I never knew exactly how this message had been conveyed. His surgeon was a beautiful, tall, dark-haired woman from North Carolina whose brisk manner with everyone but him was daunting. He trusted and respected her and had established from the beginning that all medical information about his condition would come directly from her to him. It was, in the end, very brave of him, but the only way I knew exactly when she had told him was to watch his eyes. And what I saw that day I have never been able to describe.

Before that, in the midst of pain and frustration, his face had mobility of expression; the skin seemed alive and the eyes had lights in them; when you looked at him, his eyes looked back at you. But that morning when I knew he knew, it was like a processing of information that stops all process. All day I watched his face, when I could, and I still don't know what I saw, but it was a look that had nothing to do with what it was looking at, and when I looked as far into his eyes as I could there was no end.

And what is the protocol for the moment after the announcement of death? Is that when we are to turn our backs in silence?

That day I did not dare look at you.

July 19, 1993
2:30 P.M.

Dear Alice,

After I typed my last sentence on July 15, the computer screen suddenly filled with horizontal lines and the letters of my words became enlarged, like the writing in children's school notebooks. Three vertical lines appeared on the left of the screen. No function key worked. I wondered if I had lost one or all of the letters I had written you. I turned off the computer. I waited.

After an hour I turned on the computer. This time there was one vertical line to the left. The center of the screen began to grow dim, then darken. Suddenly, the monitor went black and emitted a low cry (this was later defined as a "high frequency sound"). I had the jarring sense of being present at a kind of death, watching the dimming and then the blacking out, hearing the final cry! Never before had my computer uttered a sound.

For three days I've been unable to concentrate. The complete paralysis

Dear Alice,

After I typed "The complete paralysis," the new monitor I had borrowed went berserk. The word "paralysis" flickered and then multiplied; so did all the preceding words I had typed; then the lines of print began to march rapidly down the page. At the computer shop, I described this to a disbelieving salesman.

In order to retrieve my file, we first had to rename it. (It was called "Alice.") The man at the computer shop gave the file his own name, "Mark," and then brought up one after another of my letters to you on the screen, to demonstrate that they were safe. Nothing had been lost, but something irrevocable had happened.

My "box" of letters had been casually opened, read, and "marked." What was necessary to save my writing took it into the public realm for just a moment, but that moment changed my relationship to it entirely.

Dear Alice,

Right now the Midwest is suffering the worst floods in the history of this country. Over six million acres are inundated, causing at least five billion dollars of damage to eight states. In Des Moines, 250,000 people are without drinking water.

At 2 A.M., in the back yard outside our bedroom window, a sprinkler shoots streams of water fifteen feet into the night air. I ask David to look with me so that I will be certain it isn't a dream.

This afternoon while it is raining, I see the sprinkler again, watering the front lawn in the same fashion. I can see it more clearly now, the streams of water curving out over the soaked, scorched grass from left to right and then from right to left in regular arcs. It is a beautiful and absurd sight.

There are odder things in the world than computers that cry out as they die and words that blink at you and march away.

Dear Alice,

There are so many stories of mothers I've heard or read about: mothers who are alcoholic, absent, abusive, indifferent, overbearing, nosy, cold, bored, unwelcoming; mothers who cannot be trusted or relied on or believed, or whose admiration or praise can never be earned; mothers without compassion, tolerance, intelligence, or imagination; mothers who want you to live *their* aspirations for you rather than to live your own or who want you simply to live the lives they failed to live; mothers who tell you how often you ruined their lives or their day, who lock you out of house or heart, who don't listen and never hear, whose love is too frail to survive disappointment or the latest outrage, who secretly did not want to have children or didn't want the children they had, who lacked resilience and were simply worn down by life and the lives around them. And others: those whose hearts atrophied for perfectly understandable reasons, those who were as self-absorbed as their children, those for whom the cost of mothering was too high.

I cannot tell these stories. They are the stories most people tell.

July 25, 1993
11 A.M.

Dear Alice,

Last night at dinner David asked me if I wished that Ken and I had not sold the house after you died, but "kept it in the family." It was a painful question. This morning I dreamed my answer.

In my dream David and I, returning from a late-night walk, arrive at our third-floor apartment too quickly, as if an intervening story had vanished. The door to our newly rented, adjoining apartment is open. We go in, expecting a robbery, but instead, the rooms (which, in reality, contain only a desk and some bookcases) are *filled* with furniture. I notice an upholstered sofa, somewhat worn, not the one you last slept on. I see a small lamp shining brightly on a low table. Instantly I awake in a state of desolation.

It was the scene of my adolescence: coming home in the dark, seeing the light that signaled your loving presence. It's not the house I want or its furniture. Only that lamp waiting to be turned off for the night is what I would have wished to keep "in the family."

Dear Alice,

I have just returned from a four-day trip to Virginia. On the train going south, there was a very small African American child in the seat behind me who wanted to go home and who announced this desire with increasing volume all the way from New Haven to Washington, D.C. I could hear the mother say that other people in the train did not want to listen to yells and complaints. She tried to distract her child by pointing out the many bodies of water we passed in Connecticut, New York, Pennsylvania, Delaware, and Maryland. The child always seemed to look too late and then to want what was missed to come back into view. The grandmother, across the aisle, finally said, "Once it goes away, it doesn't come back until the next trip."

When the family first entered the train, home was just outside. Every time the train stopped, the child wanted to get out because that's where home would be. The mother's rational explanations did not alter her child's expectation. "Have you lost your mind? Haven't we had this conversation already?" she asked, and then answered herself: "This child is without logic."

As we got closer and closer to the end of the trip, the cries got louder and louder. Suddenly the child screamed, "No!" My body went limp in gratitude for a cry I understood perfectly.

Two Voices

I'd like to hear it if you would like to tell it.

THE ROOM IN WHICH WE SAT recording our two voices became your home for the last months of your life. Through the window above the sofa bed you could see the pink blossoming of your crape myrtle and the upper branches of a neighbor's tree that touched your rooftop. Beyond the sliding glass door at the back of the house, you could see your rose trellis and the raspberry bushes, and always the squirrels and birds alternating at several bird feeders. You could see the tree struck several years ago by lightning beginning to grow fresh branches and leaves. You could see the flowers and plants of other yards. Sometimes curious cats, whom you disliked, appeared on the lawn or pressed their bodies against the glass door.

This room you had moved into downstairs we called "the new room." Its interior red brick wall was originally the outer wall of the house. In "the new room," you were both "inside" and "outside," especially during heavy snow, thunderstorm, hail, and high wind when the walls seemed to fall away. That room attracted light, especially moonlight. A full moon lit up almost every corner.

One summer afternoon, listening to birdsong through the open glass door, I lay down beside you on the sofa bed. I remember saying I would be up in a minute. I remember the sweetness of the air and a cardinal in the nearest tree. An hour later, you still had not moved for fear of disturbing me.

For over a decade, I do not reenter your house or the room in which we sat. These voices are my return.

Tape #1

The first tape begins November 6, 1989.

The voices often overlap. They interrupt, continue, and finish each other's thoughts and sentences. There are supporting undersounds ("mmm-hmms"), some almost inaudible. Such small, fleeting negotiations modulate the conversations we most treasure. Alice's voice ranges from mischievous to meditative, from elegiac to ecstatic. Shifts in subject and mood occur suddenly, at times inexplicably. No particular value is placed on sequence or succinctness.

A comment or sound simultaneous with another is enclosed within slashes, for example, /Hmm/.

Susan: Can you tell me some of your earliest memories?

Alice: Well . . . I lived at first in the Bronx, and I remember a traumatic experience, if you'd like to hear that.

S: I'd like to hear it if you would like to tell it.

A: I must have been about six or seven. And I disliked milk as a child. I *was* kind of thin, and I remember my mother was told by a doctor to see that I got a milkshake every day. . . . And one day I was sent down to the corner store—we called them candy stores at that time, where they sold ice cream and milkshakes and candy and cigars and so on—and I remember going in to buy my milkshake after school. A man came in with a little cigar box. He handed it to me and said, "Would you hold this? Somebody's gonna come and get it from you in a few minutes. Thank you," and he left. I don't remember what he looked like. All I remember is that after a few minutes the police came in and asked me all sorts of questions and I remember starting to cry. I was scared. All I could tell them was that a man gave a cigar box to me and I was supposed to hold it for someone. They said thank you, and one of them went home with me, to see where I lived, I guess, and when I went inside I was so shaken I remember my mother said, "Don't bother her anymore. You can see she's nervous and upset," and she took me in and put me in my bed. Then she went out and tried to answer his questions. They did not come back anymore. But I remember the traumatic experience it left me with. Nobody really knew what those men were up to. At least I don't know.

S: Goodness [low subdued voice].

You held a box you never opened. And did it haunt you, too, for the rest of your life?

Alice: Now what else do I remember [laughs] of those days? [laughing]. I have a picture of myself and my brother in the snow. A stranger had come up to take our photograph, and I remember both of us were kind of frightened of strangers. He said [deep voice], "Well, I just want to take your picture," and, "Where's your mother?" We said she was in the store, and he waited. When she came out, he told her that was his job: he was a street photographer and had taken a picture of us in this deep snow and perhaps she'd like to buy it, it would be ready next week. As a matter of fact, she bought it and it's one of my fondest [pause] memories. I have that picture which I love [a tender, musical voice].

Susan: Yes, it's a beautiful picture.

A: Yes. I must have been about seven, or less, and my brother was a year and a half younger. We're very solemn in the picture [S laughs].

In the Snow, William and Alice Parson.
New York City, c. 1920.

I look again at the framed sepia photograph you gave me of you and your brother standing near a packed wall of snow outside a grocery store in the Bronx, waiting for your mother. Bill is wearing a well-cut, belted winter coat over dark slacks; he is holding a small shovel. His eyes look wistful, even a little dreamy, as if he is imagining the inner workings of the camera before him. You are elegance itself: shoulder-length hair under a light-colored beret, white tights, dark coat with a large fur collar, black shoes with high tops and laces. Your eyes are deep, dark, far apart, under perfectly formed eyebrows. The eyelids are partly closed: a woman's eyes in a child's face.

Now I look more closely at the photograph and notice for the first time signs of trouble in your beautiful eyes and around your brother's mouth.

Alice: What else do I remember? After that I remember my father owning a small delicatessen store, in the Bronx. I went to P.S. 53. I guess I was a pretty smart child. I got various prizes, including one from the principal, Mr. Henwood. I have that book now.

Susan: Do you remember what the prize was for?

A: Yes. We had eight years in elementary school. I had been skipped two years' worth of schooling, so I was only twelve when I graduated [from eighth grade]. In that last year, we had decided that I would go to Hunter College High School. In order to get in, you had to take tests in arithmetic and in English. I believe I got a 99.8 as a total. My principal was very proud of me and said it was the highest grade any student in his school had ever gotten. So he gave me a copy of *Joan of Arc*.

S: That's very appropriate [both laugh].

A: So in September I started at Hunter College High School. It was very competitive; all the kids in that high school were the cream of the cream. But there was something I didn't like about it. We had many classes to take. I don't think that would have bothered me. It was an all-girls school. I don't know that that *would* have bothered me—I was never very social-minded. Shortly after September we moved. My father had bought a candy store in Brooklyn.

S: You were now twelve?

A: I was twelve, just entering high school. And I had to take a train to go to school. And I remember not doing too well on the train. I was carsick. It was a little rough on me, so my parents agreed that I should not continue at Hunter College High School. They transferred me to Erasmus Hall High School. . . . We lived in Flatbush, at that time, and Erasmus Hall was a good high school with a good reputation. In any event, I *loved* it. It was co-ed and it was not as competitive and I don't believe I had as many classes to take [pause]. But I know I loved it, and I was so relieved at never having to *travel* in the subway to school; I always appreciated that [slowly]. Now we lived behind the store.

S: Do you remember the street?

A: On Church Avenue in Brooklyn. It was the corner of Church and Argyle /S: Umm-hmm. Umm-hmm/.

S: I've been there.

A: Ohh.

S: I went to find the place where you lived.

A: And was it still a /S: It was a . . . / a candy store when you saw it?

S: No, but I saw the location.

A: There was a whole block of stores. I remember it [voice suddenly very tired]. Outside of our street of stores was a very lovely residential area. But I of course didn't live in any of those houses [voice strong again]. I lived behind the store in a small apartment /S: Hmm-hmm/ attached to the store.

S: Umm-hmm [pause]. Can you describe the apartment? The rooms?

A: We always entered through the store. Behind the store, there was a little narrow area for storage, as I remember it, and we went through that into our living room. Beyond the living room, there was a dining room /S: Mmm/ and then one bedroom /S: Mmm/. To the right of the bedroom was a kitchen /S: Mmm-hmm/ and a bathroom /S: Mmm-hmm/, and we were lit by a shaft that gave light to the rooms that surrounded it: the living room, which was my brother's bedroom during the night, and the dining room [Alice's bedroom] and the bathroom, all were lit that way. The kitchen had an outdoor entrance to an alley and the bedroom also had light from the alley. So we [pause] were very comfortable there. I knew no better. It was perfectly all right with me [small laugh] /S: Mmm-hmm/.

I am struck by the resonant image of a single shaft of light that lit everything around it.

Alice: All of the rooms had windows onto a *shaft* of light /S: Oh/. The only outside *light* came from the *shaft* /S: Oh/. You didn't look out onto any pretty places /S: Hmm-mmm/. None of our windows did. Even the *real* window in the bedroom just looked out onto an areaway. But on the other side of that areaway was a laundry and behind that laundry lived my first boyfriend and his family, so

Susan: [Interrupting] Oh!

A: Yeah [both laugh]. Not too much of a . . . [partly inaudible, covered by laughter]. Oh, I guess it could have been something . . . but . . . [A laughs; then S laughs].

Listening again to the first tape, I notice unexpected pauses, sudden changes in tonal quality, the ebb and flow of vocal strength, the moments when one of us chooses to wait out or fill up a pause. In the sounds of these voices, in their intimate exchanges of tempo and timbre and energy, there is another story lost in the telling.

Your voice has now become a text. I wish I could have studied it this way long ago.

Susan: Did you make friends at Erasmus?

Alice: I made friends rather quickly. My bosom friends were Bea Filler, Madeline Levin, Flossie Fishkin, and Dottie Weisberger. Those are their maiden names. [I know all these women by their married names: Beatrice Taruskin, Madeline Early, Florence Shapiro, and Dorothy Fishkin.] I made many other friends who were in my classes, but these were really my bosom friends. They didn't live close, around the corner, but we met often [pause]. Madeline especially used to have things on her mind very often. She would come over in the afternoons and we would take *long walks.* We were only a block from the Parade Grounds and then Prospect Park.

S: Were there concerts in Prospect Park at that time?

A: [Small low voice] No. Just lovely green places to walk [voice suddenly tired], and ball fields all over. The Parade Grounds was a large open area, much like the Washington Mall here, where games were played [voice very tired].

S: And you and Madeline walked there and talked?

A: Yes.

S: Or you listened and Madeline talked?

A: Mostly that [both laugh]. But if I ever went walking, that's where I'd walk, just a block down Argyle to the Parade Grounds. . . . That's where I got all my greenery [long pause]. And in high school [pause], I did well, as I said [brief laugh]. I liked school.

I remember having one Latin teacher who made me love Latin. I don't know whether it was she completely or whether it was my feeling for logic and the need to *organize* things. I felt that Latin was the most *organized* language that I had studied. I used to *love* taking tests, particularly in Latin. I'd sit there, everybody was quiet around me, and I would figure out how things *had* to fit here and things *had* to go there. I'd have to look for my nominative, *then* my verb, and so on. It was fun, to me [voice excited]. And I think that's what got me interested in becoming a Latin major later on [voice suddenly tired; a long pause]. What else?

S: Did anyone help you with your homework?

A: Not in high school. My parents did not involve themselves too much in my schooling. I don't believe we even had PTAs. During my high school days, I would be helpful to my father, I know. When I came home from school, I would send him in for his afternoon nap. My mother too had worked hard all day and was tired, so I would give them both relief. The afternoon was the quietest time in the store. I remember sitting on a kind of desk, in front of the cash register, doing my homework while I took care of the store /S: Hmm/ [pause].

Your voice carries the heavy weight of tiredness that you witnessed in your own parents. No one offers you relief.

We continue to talk and your voice recovers.

Susan: And did you work in the store in the evening?

Alice: Sometimes but not often. I think my mother took her turn [laughs] in the evening. I had the afternoon stint, as it were. My younger brother was supposed to help my father in the morning, delivering newspapers. I can't really remember how much of it he did. My father had to get up very early and he would deliver newspapers all over the area.

S: Hmmm [pause]. Hmmmm [pause].

A: So there we were. We all had chores . . . [interrupting herself]. I remember another thing I used to love about the store. Several months before Christmas you had to go downtown to big warehouses and select your Christmas merchandise. And my father started taking me with him /S: Oh/. And I *loved* that. I remember making suggestions to him [pause], like, "Oh, I think these dolls . . . would *go*, or these Christmas cards." He'd let me pick out the Christmas cards, and I'd pick the ones *I* liked. In the end, we would make all our selections and somebody there would have a pad and a pencil and take our orders and we would go home, and I was always so *proud* when the orders came in and I'd see the things he selected on my recommendation [voice very happy; laughs]. Not everything, of course [both laugh; long pause].

I remember Christmas. It was *fun*. We had to make room in the store somehow; I remember setting out big boards, and it was like being a decorator. We would have to set things up and put all our new merchandise [voice strong], and *Christmas* merchandise, first on these tables and then where the shelves were, and [pause] I helped a lot with that. I really liked it. We'd have a section where the Christmas cards were set out. So I took great pride in how much Christmas business we would do [laughs; long pause].

S: The store was open Christmas Day?

A: Oh yes. Oh yes. Definitely Christmas Day. People would come in and say, *"Oh,* what am I going to buy?" and I'd sell them all *kinds* of things [voice stronger]. If they'd forgotten something for wife, daughter, or mother, I'd find things to sell them. We even had watches and I remember little knives that were pretty that I used to urge on people. And yes, oh *yes,* Christmas Day was very busy [pause].

S: Well, what was the *name* of the store?

A: Had no name [playfully].

S: Had no name?

A: Just the corner candy store which carried *many* things. We didn't have big Drug Fairs and supermarkets in those days. Our neighbor was just a *grocer;* next to him was *the* butcher.

S: Mmm, I see, I see.

A: And we were the candy store. We did not sell drugs or big items. But we had a mixture of things, as I remember. Magazines. I read most of my magazines just standing in front of the magazine rack [S laughs]. We had newspapers out in front. And there was a cigar counter. We sold a lot of cigarettes and cigars. And then we had a big ice box for ice cream. We called it a "dry candy store" because we did not sell sodas. We had only ice cream, which I re-

The Candy Store on Church Avenue, Anna and Alice Parson [?].
Brooklyn, no date.

member ladling into containers—quarts or pints or gills [a gill is a
quarter pint].

S: [Pause.] It sounds as if you were happy.

A: [Strong voice:] *I* feel as if I had a happy childhood because I
was *always loved* by my parents and my brothers, and [pause] I really
must have felt as if I was the only child or the eldest child. I *was* the
only daughter, it's true, the only *girl* in the family. But I just have a
feeling that I felt *important*. I felt my self-worth [brief pause] at all
times.

*I ask about your father, who died when you were thirty-two and I was
four.*

Susan: Do you think that feeling of importance partly came from your father's trusting you as . . . as a business associate?

Alice: Good question, because I do think that's so. He gave me any self-confidence I ever needed [brief pause]. I never even asked for an allowance, as I remember it, because he would say, "You don't need an allowance. You need *money*? Take it" [S laughs]. He had *complete* faith in me, and I would take what I thought I needed for the day and that was about all. I needed money for school, particularly later on when I went to college. We were still living in this apartment all through my college days, too [long pause].

S: Your father probably . . . gave more money to his children [slowly] than he saved for himself, for his own needs.

A: Yes . . . yes. He was an immigrant of the kind you read so much about, the Jews who *fled* from Russia for one of various reasons. In his case, it was probably poverty more than anything else, because he was one of seven children, I believe, in a very poor family. And one by one, they came here. First the oldest, and then he and others followed. And six of them came. [The other five were David, Sarah, Rachel, Judel, and Ben.] He and the rest of his family never had much of a formal education because of where they lived or for other reasons that I don't know of [voice more musical]. So when he came here at what I think was about age seventeen, he immediately looked for work. And I don't really know—and I'm very sorry that I never asked questions [pause]—I don't *know* much about his background [pause]. . . .

I have unearthed my grandfather's certificate of death, looking for what it might offer "about his background." He died at 806 Monterey Street in Coral Gables, Florida, on July 29, 1944, at 8:39 A.M. The immediate cause of death is "heart failure." The physician who signed the certificate is William Parson, M.D., of 806 Monterey Street, Coral Gables—his son.

Despite a stern warning in the left margin—"This is a permanent record. Every item of information should be carefully provided"—four ques-

tions about the deceased remain unanswered. In the space after "Father's Name," "Father's Birthplace," "Mother's Maiden Name," and "Mother's Birthplace," a single word— "unobtainable"—is typed four times.

In missing Alice, I discover so many more missing persons.

Alice: But I do know that what my father wanted in life was to get enough money to send his children to college and give them a *strong* education [spoken slowly with particular force]. And that meant in our family that both my brothers became doctors and I was to become a teacher [pause].

Joyce Carol Oates speaks of "those penumbral states of consciousness that do, in the long run, constitute our lives." [1] There are events in your life that remain in complete shadow. Your father's death is one of them. Whenever I have mentioned that loss to you, tears fill your eyes and I do not press you for words.

Susan: But whose idea was it that you become a teacher?

Alice: I don't know. I think it was just *expected* of any bright *girl* student: she was to become a teacher. Any bright *boy* student was to become a doctor or a lawyer [laughs]. . . . And you just . . . *I* didn't question it. I just *knew* I was to go to college and then become a teacher. And since I loved school, I never thought anything else [slight embarrassed laugh].

S: When did you get to see your family *together*? If you were all taking shifts at the store, was there any "family time"?

A: Well, there couldn't be because the store was open until 11 at night /S: Oh/. My father got up at 5 in the morning. My mother must have taken the late night shift, and then she liked to sleep late in the morning. She had a habit of not wanting to get up early. So [pause] there was really not *too* much time, except I know she cooked big dinners for us, but we had to take shifts eating it, I'm sure. . . . I do remember being *with them* in the store and in the house. We were *together,* but we all went our own ways, doing what we had to do [voice strong], but I felt as if it was *family* all the time [voice strong; long pause].

And when I went to college, remember, I was still working in the store—[pause] probably even more because I was older then. . . . *Oh,* you know I went to Hunter College, finally. I took the exams to get in and was admitted, so that meant no tuition for my parents. And I had a Regents Scholarship, which was based on our grades in the Regents tests given each year in New York to the high school students. If you got certain grades, you got $100 a year: big deal [both laugh]. That $100 I gave to my father toward my college education.

S: Well, that's very impressive. How many of those awards were made each year?

A: I don't know. I think Dad also got one.

S: And how was it decided that you would go to Hunter?

A: I think I did not *push* to go away from home [pause]. Maybe [voice very tired] I had the inclination to stay there, or the feeling that I was *needed,* or perhaps just the feeling that I was *not* going to be a burden because they still had to send my younger brother to medical school. And my younger brother got to go to the *best* medical school [Columbia Presbyterian], the most expensive, in the area [laughing voice], and they needed money.

I ask if you still had motion sickness traveling to Hunter College on the subway each day.

Alice: Physically, it was bad. I mean I was still very carsick and I had to devise all sorts of ways I would not be carsick. Number one, I *never* could *read* in the train /S: Mmm/, so I couldn't spend that hour doing homework or catching up /S: Mmm/. Number two, I learned [laughs] that if I got in the front car, for some reason or other, and stood and looked out at the tracks straight ahead of me, I could avoid nausea [pause]. So that is [slight pause] what I did. [Pause.]

Nausea played a disproportionate role in your early life: first, the transfer out of Hunter College High School and then the loss of hundreds of hours of reading time during college. But at least you found a thing you could do. Later, with the crushing nausea of chemotherapy, you never found a front car with a view of the tracks straight ahead.

Now I ask about your extracurricular activities at college and learn that your three-and-a-half-year experience in student government may have set a lifelong pattern.

Alice: Well, it seems as if I was destined to be in the administrative end always [voice vigorous; S laughs]. . . . I was the student council representative, then class president, and I must have been student council representative again until the last year. My senior year I was elected [brief pause] secretary of the student council. Hmm, I ought to check this in my yearbook. But I do know I was on student council all those years. And, now that I think of it, that's the sort of existence I've followed all my life: I've been in an administrative position but *never* wanted the top job.

Susan: But you *were* the top job. You were class president.

A: All right, let me tell you about that [both laugh]. The president of our class was a girl whom I *adored*. She was a *tall,* beautiful, blonde, Scandinavian girl named Lily Gundersen. She was the sweetest, most charming girl I had met. And when after a time she did not want to be president—I must have had a job in her administration—she said, "You've got to do it," so I ran for office. And I found that when I was president, I could not sit still for mediocre work [the last two words equally stressed and carefully enunciated]. I don't think I was trying to compete with Lily. She had a different style. But, for example, we had to have a class party, and [laughs; pause] I remember having people making posters: "Alice says this," and "Alice says that" and "Alice says, 'You all come'" [laughing voice; S laughs].

We had a theme of "Alice in Wonderland," and eventually our class party was so jam-packed it was ridiculous. We had to turn people away, it was so well-attended, and it was *all,* I know, because of the work I put in and the *publicity* [laughs] I created, and after that I said, "I don't want to do this. I create an overkill." I don't know why I felt that way, but I felt that [voice more serious] about my management . . .

S: Style?

A: . . . "style," thank you. And so this was not where I should be. I should be in a much bigger place if I was going to do this, and I didn't want to do it again. I felt the place I belonged was in the student council where I could present my ideas and so forth, and I didn't want to be class president any more [wan laugh] /S: Mmm-hmm/. So that's how that came about [small sigh], and I remember it very distinctly [long pause].

I listen again to your voice on the tape saying, "I should be in a much bigger place if I was going to do this," and I wonder what that might have been.

I listen to us in memory now, looking at words.

Susan: Weren't you also in the Sing Club?

Alice: [With excitement] Oh, the Sing was one of the activities [every syllable pronounced crisply] of Hunter College. I don't know if they're still doing it. It was a famous tradition; every year each class would compete against the other classes. . . . We would

COLLEGE LEADER

News Clipping,
Alice Parson.
February 28, 1932.

ALICE PARSON

Miss Parson, of 1303 Church ave., a Hunter College senior, has been very much in the limelight at the college as a result of her extra-curricular activities.

Miss Parson was a council representative in her first semester at Hunter. She was vice president of her upper freshman class and president of her class in her sophomore year. In her junior year she was a council representative and chairman of the sing committee. At present she is secretary of the student council, chairman of the classification system and chairman of the central sing committee.

In the recent controversy that arose over the Bulletin, the Hunter weekly, Miss Parson rose to the occasion by helping the student council publish the emergency edition.

have a Sing Committee, and there were some really brilliant people making up songs and some brilliant designers. I was not on the Sing Committee, no, I was busy with other facets of the college, but I went each time and I was part of Sing. [A news clipping, dated February 28, 1932, states, perhaps mistakenly, that Alice Parson was "chairman of the central sing committee."] It took *hundreds* of us [pause]. . . . We rehearsed at Carnegie Hall or the Metropolitan Opera House. And I remember coming home at [pause] twelve, one o'clock in the morning [voice suddenly young and nonchalant], got off the subway about a mile from my home, and I'd walk home on Church Avenue, all the way home /S: Mmm/. Nobody ever bothered you [pause]. Oh, sometimes you'd have little pests bothering you, but basically nothing to get worried about [voice very low, almost inaudible].

S: Well, one question I forgot. Did you ever take an aspirin? [A laughs].

I know you are responding to a family joke about your antipathy to almost all medicines, but I cannot transcribe that sudden burst of laughter. I listen over and over: there is nothing like it anywhere else on the tapes. Your laughter comes from an unrecoverable source, an intimate exchange of energy in that room. It is inexplicably moving, this mysterious sound of pure pleasure.

Alice: I think I mentioned to you that in our family, as I recall, we had very little illness. And I don't remember [pause] taking pills. I do remember something, now. Probably when I was twelve, after we moved to that Church Avenue address, I remember my mother had some severe asthma attacks, and sometimes she had to go to bed, it was so bad—/S: Mmm-hmm/, and I remember having her teach me from her bed [pause] how to make chicken dinner /S: Oh/ [A laughs]. I remember I would go next door to Mr. Springer's [hearty voice] grocery and buy my vegetables, and I guess I'd go down to Mr. Ring's butcher shop and get a chicken and she would tell me how to clean that chicken. We didn't get them nicely cleaned the way you do nowadays. And I would have to singe the feathers off the chicken. We didn't cut it up. She taught me to make chicken soup with the chicken, so, actually, boiled chicken in soup . . . is one of the first things I ever learned to make [long pause]. What was I supposed to be talking about?

Susan: Well, no, you *answered* that question. It was: "Did you ever take an aspirin?" [laughs].

A: [Serious] Oh, *aspirin,* and then I remembered my *mother* was the one who had a serious case of asthma. . . .

How sad it now seems that you feel you must account for having fallen into a reverie about your mother and must fit answers to questions.

Susan: Did you teach yourself to cook, except for the chicken lesson?

Alice: Maybe this is why I don't enjoy cooking: I remember in the sixth grade we had to take *cooking* and the only things I remember being taught to cook were how to boil onions [both laugh]— was that ever *awful!*—and also how to make chocolate puddings [S laughs]. And . . . [more serious tone] now this may be a confession coming up here. It seems to me I did not know [talks slowly] how to [pause] light an oven. Or perhaps I had never been *allowed* to light the oven with a match. And I remember one day my class was sent to Grand Central Palace in New York City . . . our *cooking class* was on display! I remember not knowing how to light that oven and I was so *ashamed.* And somehow I managed to inveigle one of the other kids to light the oven . . . pretending my hands were too full [S laughs; A doesn't]. We had to light the oven with a match and I didn't know how to light it [voice weakens; S laughs encouragingly]. Anyway, those horrible boiled onions remain with me to this day [S laughs].

I listen to the tape. Your voice is sadder than I had remembered, and under my laughter I now hear for the first time a small sigh. Why is this "confession coming up here"? Why didn't I say that it is no shame not to know something we have to be taught to know? And why didn't I say that the teacher of a cooking class should teach students how to light an oven with a match? And why did only I laugh?

Susan: You became politically active later in life. Can you say anything about the political activities or interests of your family?

Alice: Well, my father *was* a socialist [pause]. As I understand, he was running away from the Bolshevik communist regime. And I don't know how much he was involved in the underground work in Russia before he came, but he came here as a socialist and so [pause] in my high school days I guess I started [pause] making friends with people [pause] who went to socialist rallies and clubs. I do remember going to places where Norman Thomas was speaking on the street corners. I seem to remember the street corner platforms that were built /S: Hmm/ and a lot of us young high school and college students would be the claque. We would make the noise and applaud and so on. I remember the name Judge Jacob Panken [at that time, a Socialist judge in New York]. I don't remember what we did for *him* [long pause]. I do remember some little groups and organizations. . . .

A telephone rings in the background; the tape recorder clicks off and clicks on again. A new topic emerges.

SOCIETY OF FRIENDS OF
THE WORKMEN'S CIRCLE SCHOOLS
175 East Broadway, New York 2, N. Y.

№ 46956 G

MEMBERSHIP CARD

_____, 194__

Received from_____

Address _____

$1 the sum of ONE DOLLAR for membership dues for 1946-7
Note: You are not a member until you receive official membership card from central office of the Society. $1

The Society of Friends of the Workmen's Circle schools exists for the purpose of raising funds for the Workmen's Circle Schools to assure their proper functioning.

The aid of all members is requested in the membership campaign.

For the last six years the Society distributed the sum of $19,000 (from $5 to $1000) to 756 members for their active participation in the campaigns of 1940-41-42-43-44-45-46.

During February, 1947, the following "Matonos" in U. S. Victory Bonds will be distributed in the amount of $4,000.00 to 143 members.

1 "Matono"	$1,000.00	15 "Matonos" each	$50.00
2 "Matonos" each	200.00	30 "Matonos" each	25.00
5 "Matonos" each	100.00	30 "Matonos" each	10.00
	60 "Matonos" each $5.00		

Please keep this card and compare with official membership receipt.

Entertainment   Dancing

Rebel Arts Night
ONE-ACT PLAY   CHALK TALK
POETRY READING

FLATBUSH SOCIALIST CLUB
2239 Church Avenue, Brooklyn
Bet. Flatbush & Bedford Aves.

Saturday Evening, March 18, 1933

Admission 35 cents   (Proceeds for Rebel Arts Murals)

Workmen's Circle Schools, Manhattan 1946;
Rebel Arts Night, Brooklyn 1933.

Susan: I wonder if you ever saw your parents reading a book or having time to read a book?

Alice: I never saw much time for sitting and reading. But I *know* my *mother* [pause] must have read. She had periods where she was supposed to go in and rest, and I do believe she read then. My mother actually had a very fine educational and cultural background; she knew a great deal and had read a great deal before she came to this country. She also had a great love of culture and *music.* We had a piano in that cluttered Brooklyn dining room, did I mention that?

S: No.

A: We had a piano, and we all took piano lessons, and [musical voice returns] I don't remember ever seeing my mother play, but she *loved* music. I'm trying to think if we had a phonograph, because I feel as if I had music in my home. . . . I know my mother occasionally, not very often to be sure, went to the opera by herself. Her English was pretty good, but I don't think she went to theater much [pause]. And I really don't remember what books she read.

I know my father read newspapers voraciously, the English *and* the Jewish newspapers. Whether he read books I couldn't say. But he had all these papers and magazines in the store, and he would read them [pause]. We kids, of course, read what we had to because of school. I [pause] don't remember being *pushed* into cultural events, but [pause] when I had an occasion to be invited out, I would choose a play.

The careful phrasing juxtaposes the passive infinitive ("to be invited out") and the active voice ("I had an occasion"; "I would choose a play"), with its sly assertion of self-chosen pleasure.

Three Sisters under an Umbrella: Anna (top), Basia, and Masha Levitt. Grodno, no date.

Anna Levitt's Mother (name unknown). Grodno, no date.

Anna Levitt's Father (name unknown). Grodno, no date.

Alice: One of the things I remember is the Fourteenth Street Theater, Eva Le Gallienne's theater, the Civic Theater it was called. I remember a number of plays with Eva Le Gallienne and her group, *wonderful* plays. I believe I even saw Walter Hampden doing *Cyrano de Bergerac* [S laughs with pleasure; pause]. I think I went to the opera once, and for the life of me now I can't remember whether my mother took me or who *went* with me [pause].

Susan: Do you remember which opera?

A: Yes, I do [voice suddenly vigorous again]. It was a double feature: *Cavalleria* and *I Pagliacci*. . . . Maybe Leon went [pause] with me. Anyhow . . .

S: [Quickly] Who was Leon?

A: Leon's the boyfriend from the laundry.

S: *Ohh.* [A laughs.] He was a *cultured* boyfriend [a laugh in S's voice].

A: He grew up to be a teacher, in New York high schools [pause]. I don't know whether it was his idea or mine, but that's the one time I went to the opera, that double feature.

S: Do you remember your first date? Where you went on your first date?

A: No, I can't remember those things [voice low; pause]. It *might* have been this, because I do remember. . . .

(Tape #1 ends here.)

William Trevor is right: "the romantic past [of our parents] can only be guessed at, and all such curiosity invariably comes too late."[2]

Tape #2

The second tape was recorded shortly after the first one, on November 6, 1989. It begins in the middle of a conversation about witch hazel, whose scent has stirred up a memory of an event from half a century ago.

Susan: And it seems that witch hazel is connected with Leon at the laundry? [Laugh in S's voice.]

Alice: [Laughs. Wonderful laugh.] Not necessarily Leon. But it made me think of the fact that while I was in high school, people who would come into the store got to know me, and one time a lady came in and asked me if I would tutor her son in math. He was failing algebra. So this was one of my first paying jobs. I used to go over to his home at a certain time in the afternoon to do his algebra lessons with him. One very cold winter day, after it had snowed badly, the porch was icy and I didn't realize it. As I was entering the house, I slipped and fell on the snow and ice and, though I didn't know it then, I broke a little bone in my wrist. As I remember it, I said, "Oh, I guess I'm all right," and I stayed and gave him his lesson and went on home. But by the time I got home, my wrist was quite swollen. We were not used to going to doctors and, as I remember it, my mother put witch hazel all over my wrist, to take down the inflammation, I believe, and then we made a kind of a sling for my arm and I kept it quiet. It seems to me that I had a date for that evening, and I believe it was that opera. I felt it was *very* important; I might have given up anything else, but a date like that should not be broken. I remember going. . . , smelling of pungent witch hazel, which I tried to hide. When I got to the opera, I remember wrapping a sweater and my coat around my sling [S laughs] to keep the odor down. It probably worked [S laughs].

As in the first tape, your opening story "leads" into a memory of a precious object still in your possession.

Alice: Incidentally, that leads me to remembering that I had one other paying tutoring job in my later years of high school when I was probably fifteen or sixteen. A lovely young lady who spoke very poor English came into the store. She was Russian. And she asked if I would tutor her in English.

Susan: Now how did she happen to ask *you*?

A: I don't know why these people came to me. Perhaps they had seen me in the store, spoken to me, decided I was smart enough to teach them [pause]. I agreed to go there. I remember she lived two streets down in an apartment house. I would go there, perhaps two times a week, and teach her a little bit about English grammar and then have her *read* to me, which is really what she wanted more than anything else. She wanted to hear me talk English, she wanted to talk English back to me, and to read and have me correct her pronunciation [voice hoarse but all five syllables are equally distinct]. At the time I remember she wanted to pay me and I . . . [coughs; pause].

S: This was the beginning of your many refusals to take money for the work you do?

A: [Laughs.] Could be. I really did not want to take money from her, and so I said I'd make a deal, that I would teach her English if she would teach me Russian. [Vigorous voice.] She helped me buy a small Russian book and actually in the short time I was with her, which was *less* than six months before her husband was recalled to Russia and she had to leave me—both of us were tearful [laughs] at the time—she eventually felt so obligated to me she would think of all kinds of nice things to do. Usually, when I came, she would have some Russian specialty for lunch and that's when I first tasted blini [pronounces this word with relish]—I loved them—and then she helped buy me my old Underwood typewriter, which I still have today. She was able to get me that at cost from the Amtorg, the Russian-American trading corporation . . . so I remember her [meditative tone] with great pleasure.

If I had known this story, if I had known what precious cargo Joey was pulling as we sped around that corner in my red wagon, would I not have held on to it with all my might?

As the years passed, you were the only one in the family who wanted to hold on to that Underwood typewriter. I groaned in frustration at its old-fashioned slowness. But for you it must always have recalled some blini, a Russian lady, and the heritage you recovered in her house.

Where is your Underwood now? Have I let go of it again?

Susan: . . . I don't really have a sense of how you got interested in some of the things you got interested in. *Theater,* or . . .

Alice: Theater? That's funny. I remember now. I must have some desire to be in theater deep within me.

After your death, I received a letter describing you as a counselor at Camp Mount Joy when you were seventeen: "She was by far the most creative the camp ever had. One of my most impressive recollections of her creativity was her directing and producing Humperdinck's Hansel and Gretel *. . . outdoors! She chose a beautiful meadow with a natural stage setting, coached the children with their lines and songs, created the costumes, directed the [construction of] the stage sets, kept our music counselor on the ball, and in sum gave to that camp perhaps its most memorable dramatic performance."[3] All this makes perfect sense. But you have a different story to tell about your relation to theater.*

Alice: I remember one time, in high school, a friend of mine wanted to audition for a play. She didn't want to go alone and she begged me to come with her. "I don't want to go." "Well, just sit with me" [changing her voice]. I sat in the *back row* and I remember when she was called up, she had to read something. Shortly after that, the teacher who was auditioning pointed at me and said [changing her voice: rushed and impatient]: "Come on now, let's hear you. We haven't much more time. Just you and a few others and we're going." I was too shy to decline, so I went up on stage and read something and when it was all over she asked *me* [laughs] to join the Drama Club and my poor friend Ruth was out in the cold. I don't know if she ever forgave me [S laughs].

Susan: Did you like the feeling of being on the stage?

A: Yes and no. I think my shyness was very evident then. But my voice was pretty good. They all admired my voice and my diction. I had a soft voice, and I had to be taught how to project it. But, basically, I was too shy. In fact, in the senior play I did have a part in which I had to scream. I could not, I would not [voice vigorous], scream. And I recall [laughs] that there was a young man—he was a great big guy, he was one of our football stars at Erasmus—who had a part in the play and he just seemed to *love* acting. When I said, "I can't," he said, "I'll scream for you. You just turn around." And that's what happened [S laughs]. When it came time for me to scream, I turned away from the audience. He let out a yell [A laughs] in as babyish a voice as he could [both laugh]. That was the senior play.

With a shock I realize I have never heard you scream, not in anger nor in pain. You didn't scream when they told you your beloved brother Rudy had died or when the visiting nurse assured you that Dad's warm body had no "life" left. What sound did you make when your father died? My brother remembers hearing you cry the morning your mother died, in my bedroom, three years later; I wasn't there.

I ask you to tell me about some important influences in your life: events, people, accidents. Your answer is not what I had expected.

Alice: I don't know, Sue [audible loss of energy]. I realize that I have a [pause] strange philosophy of life that [pause] whatever is going to happen is going to happen and I am almost fatalistic in the sense that I let the fates direct what I'm going to do, where I'm going, and I don't know, then, that I could . . . point out special things. They all just happened /S: Umm-hmm/.

I have just written a letter terminating your and my last joint account in a Virginia bank, a three-year certificate of deposit. On the back of the receipt I read, "Alice Letzler + Susan Cole: Matures Aug. 25, 1990."

The date of your death in your own handwriting startles me. Your voice on the tape now sounds so very weak that I am surprised we were able to continue. But we do, no matter how weary you become. That was the pattern we had learned to live with in order to live every moment we had.

One of the "highlights" (my word) of high school, you tell me, was the Journalism Club, and in your journalism class you and other students took turns editing the school paper, The Dutchman. *You wrote a weekly newspaper column with your friends Madeline and Bea, becoming, you say with a laugh, MAB: "We had to fill that column every week and we did have to dig up 'dirt,' some of which was not actually factual."*

You speak once more of how you learned to appreciate "the orderliness of Latin, the way the parts of speech had to fit a certain pattern." "You had to know the endings," you tell me.

You mention again that you loved Latin tests, the sitting "quietly" in a room where you were "able to concentrate," as if that weren't often possible in the circumstances of your growing up.

Then, in a sudden burst of energy, you launch a new story about Latin:

Alice: I remember one day when no one appeared in our Latin class. The class was getting noisier and noisier, and something made me get up in front of that class and say, "I could teach this class." I had them turn to what we were translating that day—it may have been a piece from Caesar—and I called on different people and they *responded,* and I got this wonderfully warm feeling that comes from

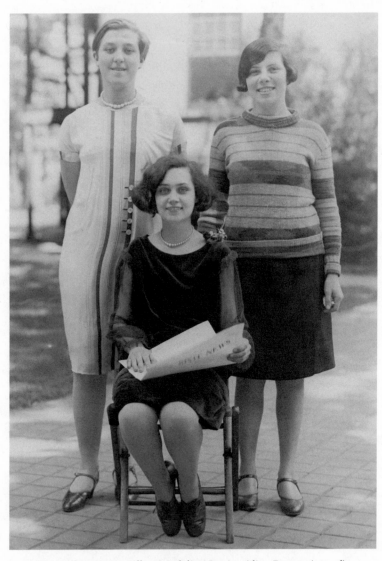

"MAB": Beatrice Filler, Madeline Levin, Alice Parson (seated).
Brooklyn, 1928.

teaching, and having people listen to you, because these were good kids and they didn't mind my doing it. They responded beautifully and I enjoyed teaching that class. I went on to major in classics when I got to college.

In giving yourself permission to retell a story, you tell me a story you never told before.

Susan: And it just happened?
Alice: It just happened.

I ask again about "important influences" in your life.

Alice: . . . I guess the biggest experience that influenced my life was that my friend Madeline had a brother-in-law who owned a children's camp and she asked me one time if I'd like to work in that camp in the summer. This was the year I was sixteen. It was when we both graduated from high school, and we went up and were waitresses there. And that's where I met Alfred who later became my husband. So I guess that was a *big* "influence."
Susan: I think so [A laughs].
A: Yeah, that's when I met him [pause], at Camp Mount Joy [voice softens].

I wait, but there are no further revelations.
You wonder why you "can't think of more things to tell" from your high school days, and you begin to talk about your brother Bill.

Alice: Bill was a year and a half younger than I. At Erasmus, he was very much a leader. He was president of the student council, in the honor society, on the debate team. He was obviously a gifted young man. I don't remember too much about his relationship with me in high school. [Correspondence with Bill reveals a similar lacuna.] I don't remember our competing. I remember as a little child when we took piano lessons, he got way ahead of me in no time and I remember at that time being set back; I refused to take lessons again and he continued for about five years.

Susan: "Set back"?

A: I mean I stopped playing piano.

S: You mean emotionally you felt set back?

A: Perhaps. I think it was because here was my younger brother outdoing me in the piano. So I quit. I never played the piano again. . . . Except for that one experience when I remember feeling outdone by him, I don't remember being jealous of him.

Now you speak of your other brother.

Alice: Rudy was a half brother. We had the same father, but his mother died shortly after he was born. He was eight years older than I. I just remember that he really—I hate to use the word, but he seemed to adore me. I was like a little doll in the family and he didn't hide it, he just liked me, and perhaps he didn't like his little brother as much as he liked me. So we had a great relationship.

I remember when he was older, he was trying very hard to make money to go to college. He had set his mind on becoming a doctor, even though at first nobody thought he should. In fact, I believe they thought he ought to be an engineer. But he wanted to be a doctor and he was determined. He was trying to save money for it, and I remember one summer he was a motorman: he learned to drive trolleys. Made good money that way. I remember one summer he worked on a farm. And working on that farm he got infested with lice. . . . When he came home, my mother recognized it, and I remember how he had to have all his hair shaved off. . . . I remember when he came home without his hair, I went into a room and I cried and cried [laughs a little; S murmurs in sympathy], and that's one memory I have of [pause], you know, how I loved him.

And [pause] I don't remember any *special* feelings with my mother. I mean I guess I was a dutiful daughter. I don't remember *ever* having set-tos [serious conflicts?] with her. I think of her as a rather private person and I never asked questions and nowadays I wish I had. . . .

I wish I had asked if "special" meant "especially negative" or "out-of-the-ordinary." So much is hidden by three generations of reticence.

Alice: In fact, if there's any culture in me [all this said in a rush], perhaps that was the influence from *her* forebears. Her family evidently were very cultured and tending towards the art world. One is a sculptor, one is a musician, one was a movie producer, and so on. . . . But I didn't know them too well. Maybe it was because she lived this [pause] quiet life where she was not sociable or maybe she couldn't, maybe she didn't want to, be sociable because she didn't have a nice home to bring people to.

Susan: And do you think your mother was happy? [pause]. You present yourself to many people as a buoyant person [A laughs].

A: It's hard to say. I think she was, certainly she was, more withdrawn than I am.

My mother's mother is a woman whom I don't recall liking. I cannot remember her ever smiling, yet in one old photograph she smiles at me with closed lips as she holds me in her lap.

I only remember two things about her before she died of the cancer that killed you and puts me at risk.

I was sitting on the floor, carelessly drawing in a coloring book with my crayons; my grandmother pointed out that I should be coloring within the lines.

The other thing I remember is riding my tricycle in our apartment and accidentally bumping into her knee. She slept, and then died, in the other bed in my room. I never missed her, and I buried whatever suspicion I may have had as a child that my accident caused her disappearance.

For the first time, we try together to imagine her life before either of us knew her.

Susan: Do you think she might have wanted to live a different kind of life . . .

Alice: [Interrupts:] Maybe. Now that we talk about it, maybe she did have a cultured background and really missed it, but she never complained in my presence. I always felt that it was she who required that we have a piano in the home.

S: And had you take piano lessons.

A: Yes. Of course [pause]. That's right. That *was* an expense, wasn't it?

S: Yes.

A: I never heard my parents quarrel about anything /S: Hmm/. She was very dutiful [the same word A used for herself as daughter]. But, as you [pause] point out now, it *may be* that she was missing things that she would have liked to have. Because she couldn't have them. My father and mother never went to social events together. . . .

S: What would you say your father's salient characteristics were?

A: I always thought of him as the most educated person I knew.

Three Generations: Susan Letzler, Anna Levitt Parson, Alice Parson Letzler.
Arlington, Virginia, October 1940.

I think he was [speaking slowly with a strong voice] self-educated; perhaps it was because he read the papers and magazines so thoroughly and was very alert when he was growing up. He could explain history and unfold current events in wonderful ways to me, so I always thought that he was the most brilliant person I knew [A laughs; S laughs], even though [strong voice] that was not [the result of] formal education. I think we had [speaks slowly again] deep mutual love [a whole new resonance, a catch in the voice], and perhaps I felt his deep appreciation of me because . . . and I hope he felt it in return [fighting tears].

S: I can't imagine his not feeling it.

A: So often I think of him more than I do of my mother and it's not fair, now that I think back [voice breaks]. I should have recognized her great qualities better, shouldn't I have?

Alice and Her Father: Alice Parson Letzler and Morris Kalman Parson.
December 1942.

How could I answer such a question? I didn't try.
Stuttering, I ask again about your father.

Susan: Well, he, he was a, he was not an impatient man, was he?

Alice: Oh no. He was patient, and loving, and [in a rush] kind and gentle and all the good things. . . . My sister-in-law Buffy has called him a saint. [Pause.] In his final days, he was at Bill and Buffy's home [long pause]. And she as a [trained] nurse probably took care of him. [Pause.]

S: Your father came here in poverty, and yet he was self-employed and he put three children through college, two through graduate education, and saw his children become doctors and teachers /A: Mmm-hmm/ and marry, and he from his own point of view must have felt that he accomplished a great deal /A: Mmm-hmm/. [There is a muffled sadness in these "mmm-hmms."] Your mother came from a different background and may have lost some of her status—

A: [A finishes S's sentence.] —by being thrown into this poor environment. *I* never knew I was poor [pause]. And I'm sorry now [voice cracks] to start thinking that maybe it did affect her, though it never affected her children.

S: [Nervously] Well, it may not have . . . affected her. I was just wondering whether you thought she was happy. But she was probably much too busy to give weather reports on her feelings.

A: True [both laugh together]. [Softer voice, as if speaking to herself:] It *is* true. And she didn't have all the wonderful time to spend or be concerned about her children individually as I do, did. . . .

I am certain I did not hear all we were saying to each other in this painful dialogue. Listening again now is like rereading a scene in a play I am preparing to teach for the first time.

Alice: I feel sad, though, now that I think back over what her life could have been [voice very unhappy, breaking a little; long pause]. But [pause] she never complained, and [a low sound of sniffing] maybe I'm making too much of it.

But you aren't. And in my attempt to know you better, I expose your pain at not really knowing your own mother.

I ask if my grandmother had any unfulfilled aspirations that you knew of, and you reply that she hadn't. I then ask the same question of you, and discover, Alice, that you and I share an unfulfilled desire to unfold the lives of our uncomplaining, deeply private mothers.

Susan: Is there any longing that you have to have done something that you now wish you had done?

Alice: No, other than that which you've just brought out, the fact now that I wish I had [pause] been closer to my *mother* to the extent that I would know more about *her* as a person and *her* aspirations. I do wish that now [sadly wistful voice; very long pause]. Okay.

Diane Arbus has said, "A photograph is a secret about a secret. The more it tells you, the less you know." [4] *Several years before you died, you gave me a set of two joined silver-framed sepia photographs. One I have always loved to look at: the picture of you and your brother standing against a bank of snow waiting for your mother. The other, a photograph of my grandmother as a young unmarried woman, I have avoided looking at closely. Now I do.*

Her face is round, her skin clear, her lips full and, I realize with a shock, almost sensual. Her hair is pulled back tightly, perhaps tied in a knot, but the severity of the style is softened by the wisps of dark hair that emerge on both sides and near the crown of the head, wisps that now seem poignant because they resemble yours when you were young and also because they seem to suggest a barely restrained impulse to break out of what binds them.

Her eyes fix me. Wherever I move, I cannot avoid their gaze and yet they seem directed straight ahead, slightly above the eye of the camera. They are neither smiling nor unsmiling, steady, intelligent, full of suppressed promise, with beautiful lights in each iris just to the left of the pupil. I look at your eyes in the adjoining photograph and put my hand across the lower part of my grandmother's face: they are the same eyes. In her face, the sensuality of

Anna Levitt.
Grodno, no date.

the full lips is held in check by the impassivity of the gaze. Something here
will not disclose itself. The more I look, the less I know.

My grandmother wears a dark old-fashioned dress with a soft, high, em-
broidered collar and full gathered shoulders whose folds masterfully catch the
light as in certain Michelangelo drawings I have seen. The bodice is tight over
a well-formed chest and an elegantly slender waist. Something has happened
to this photograph and the lower arms disappear in a cloudy white haze. For
the first time, I miss what is missing.

There are no buttons at all in the front, which gives the tightly fitted
turn-of-the-century dress a look of even more constraint. I notice something
odd: two dark chainlike pieces of fabric circle the neck, join and fall downward
together between the breasts, circling under the left breast and moving up over
it to vanish in the embellished seam near the left puffed shoulder. It looks like
a noose worn as an ornament.

Susan: What gives you pleasure or delight?

Alice: [Pause.] Nature . . . the birds and the seasons and the greenery [pause]. Mountains give me a high. They really give me a lift [voice strong]. It's hard to understand [pause]. A physical high.

S: Both your brothers lived near or on mountains.

A: That's right. They too turned to mountains and the outdoors for their enjoyment in living [pause]. That's funny, isn't it, because we were all city-bred but we evidently had a yearning to get away from it—to some extent. I mean I don't have much now, but what I have, I enjoy [lighthearted voice].

S: Let me go back for a moment. You've just graduated from college at the age of twenty. And you have to make a "choice of life." Can you remember what that felt like?

A: Well, the first thing I had to decide was, do I want to go on to graduate school? I actually *tried* at one time to enroll at Teachers College, Columbia, but somehow I didn't go through with it. I decided, "No, I don't need this. I'd better look for a job and get on with my life."

And so then I had to try to find something. And that was 1932, a very depressed year—very, very. I had taken the tests for a New York City teaching license and had gotten it, but there were no jobs to be had teaching anywhere in the city schools, so I took a civil service examination when that was offered. All of us, in my day and age, and in my bracket—that is, the young women who had gone to college expecting to be teachers—we were all in the same boat. I decided to take the civil service exam because President Roosevelt had said that he was going to attract college graduates to the government, and that meant trying to find them decent housing and getting them to come to Washington, and that appealed to me. At first I couldn't find anything. But President Roosevelt had set up different organizations to take care of the young people who couldn't find jobs even though they were college graduates. You know [playfully], WPA, PWA . . . [S laughs].

One of those organizations provided a sort of job for me. I had to go downtown and catalogue jobs. I think they did a lot of boondoggling and dreaming up things that I don't imagine were of very great use later on, and the job I had was taking people's professions and cataloguing them. I had to figure out whether, say [a twinkle in her voice], a wool-gatherer fit in the category of sheep industry or textile industry. And we had to categorize these things in certain ways, ending up with numbers, a great batch of numbers . . . [twinkle disappears], and it was boring. But I stuck with it for a while; in the meantime, I decided I should try to get a job teaching. I mentioned it to my brother Rudy, who had a medical practice in Roosevelt, Long Island, and he asked the principal of the school where he had become the school doctor if she could use me and she finally said yes, she had a fourth grade that needed a teacher. . . .

But, you tell me, "I must be getting ahead of [my] story." Before you accepted a job teaching, you worked for a time in a dry cleaning store, "pin-tagging dirty clothes."

Alice: In the evening, Al would pick me up in his car on Flatbush Avenue and take me home. He was finishing law school at Columbia and worrying about where to go, how to get a job. There were no jobs for any of us young people. Absolutely. Life was really bad in the Depression era. Finally, I did take that job in Roosevelt, Long Island, and became a fourth-grade teacher. Frankly, I disliked the disciplining that was involved because I was still young, I was rather small, short, and slender, and I was not firm enough. And I found it very difficult when I was so intent on teaching them to have to spend time as a disciplinarian.

While I was there, I used to go home every weekend to my parents. Finally, after several months of teaching, I got a telegram from Washington, asking if I would like to come to the Civil Service Commission as an examining clerk at $1,440 a year.

Susan: Was that a good salary?

A: Pretty good. That was a clerical salary. In the meantime, Al had gotten a job in Washington as an attorney with the Farm Credit Administration. [He later became assistant director of the Office of Opinion and Review at the Securities and Exchange Commission.] As an attorney, he was offered the great salary of $2,000 a year [S laughs]. So he had taken that.

Now when I got my offer in 1935, I didn't know quite what to do. I finally went to the principal of the school and told her my dilemma, told her of my offer, and asked her what I should do. I said, "I feel badly because I signed a contract to teach here." The principal, who was an unmarried middle-aged woman, looked at me and said, "If I were you, I wouldn't hesitate one moment. I would quit this job and *go*. You might meet a nice young man and your life will change and you won't be left like me."

I said, "Are you sure? I don't want to break a contract." She said, "You go." So I did.

Al was here by that time and he found a room for me—in the same boarding house as his, as a matter of fact. And life became very interesting then, because I would go my way, he would go his. In the evening, we would. . . .

(Tape #2 ends.)

Before me as I write is a crumpled, faded Western Union telegram, dated October 2, 1935:

ALFRED LETZLER＝FARM CREDIT ADMINISTRA-
TION BLDG WASHDC＝ARRIVING WITH BAGGAGE
TONIGHT AT 6 MEET ME FOR SUPPER＝ALICE

If you think you "let the fates direct" what you're going to do and where you're going, I think you're also directing those fates.

Tape #3

The last tape was recorded on November 12, 1989. The musicality of your voice, despite its great weariness, is almost always present and uncapturable. In this final tape, you decide to refer to all other family members in the third person; you consistently refer to me as "she."

The two voices again begin in the middle of a story.

Susan: Life became very interesting. How?

Alice: Well, I was now in Washington, a new, exciting city [voice dramatically more tired than in the previous tapes; enunciation equally clear and precise], and the city was full of young people of my own age and education. I really enjoyed getting to know the city and going to museums and exhibitions and everything that was available in town. And I had a lot of free time, of course. I went to work and ate meals. But other than that, my time was my own. Weekends we would go to all *sorts* of things in town, and having a boyfriend here made it easy because he would go with me,

I look again at my transcription: "he would go with me." Odd: I had misremembered it as your going to places with him. In your own text, you are at the center.

Alice [continues]: so life *was* fun and more interesting than it had been when I was trying to teach or trying to find a job to make money at home.

Susan: Well then, how did you decide to get married? It sounds as if you had a . . . perfect life.

On Board the *Trojan* to Bear Mountain,
Alice Parson and Alfred Letzler.
May 30, 1935.

A: Well, at that time, or at least in my circle, you *did* get married after a while, if you loved a man enough. [Did I hear that "enough," then?] Perhaps the question is how I *didn't* get married [S laughs] for the year and a half that I was there. And there was an answer to that.

At that time, there was a regulation, or an unwritten rule, that no more than one person in a family could be employed by the government.

Indeed, a September 27, 1935, letter to Miss Alice Parson, offering her "immediate employment" with the U.S. Civil Service Commission, adds the proviso, "If you are married and have a spouse in the government service, this offer is void."

Alice: And there may have been some sense to it because Roosevelt was trying to get work for as many young people as he could. Because of that, I didn't think we should get married at first because the salaries we were getting weren't sufficient to get a home started, find an apartment, and so on. That was what kept us not thinking about getting married for about a year and a half. . . . Sometime in 1937 that prohibition must have been lifted. So then we started talking about marriage. But there was *never* any question in our minds that we were going to be married. I must have come in '35, and we were married in May of 1937.

Susan: So you were a working wife for three years and then you became a working wife and mother.

A: That's true. I had gotten a new job. I was transferred from the Civil Service Commission to the brand new Social Security Board [pause]. Must have been an increase in salary, or, I'm trying to remember, maybe I wanted something new.

At the Social Security Board, my job was to review rules and regulations from all state departments to see if they conformed with federal regulations. I guess I was doing very well. I recall one time my chief called me in and said he wanted to recommend me to take certain courses, but he said, "I can't recommend you unless you promise me you're not going to have a child."

I got furious [strong voice]. I thought this was an intrusion into my personal life that was none of his business. I hadn't thought about it, we hadn't laid plans for that as yet, but I still didn't think he had a right to ask me to do that. And I finally said to him, "Well, I can't promise *anything* of the *sort*. I just don't *know* and I'm not going to make a decision right now. I'd rather not take that course" [voice suddenly agitated, as if reentering the experience]. "Don't spend your money on me" [A and S laugh, not a happy sound].

This is not a story you ever told me before. In college, I worried that you had given up too much for your children. Now I see what you sacrificed to protect your right to become a mother.

How many times, and in how many ways, did employers ask you and other women to make choices like this? Resisting that kind of question—are you an aspiring employee or an aspiring mother?—must have been a full-time job.

Alice: So I stayed there and I enjoyed my work and then we finally did have a child, in June of 1940. I liked my work *very* much and I was in the *midst* of preparing a manual which I didn't want to give up. I wanted to finish it, see it to its conclusion, and my boss felt I was doing a good job and didn't want me to give it up. He said, "You know, this job is yours as soon as you come back." In the meantime, I was working on that manual at home.

So, as soon as—I'm trying to remember, was it three months?— whatever maternity leave they permitted us was up, I did go back because I missed the office and the people I knew and the contacts with adults. I got a maid to stay with [pause] my baby girl [voice brightens musically], and everything worked out fine.

Susan: Did you enjoy being a mother?

A: Oh, I loved it [voice taking on more colors]. I *never* for one moment regretted the decision, and . . . she was a *pretty* baby and a *darling* baby, and a *good* baby. There was nothing not to like.

S: I understand that when this daughter was born it was very hot and you had rubber sheets [A laughs] and you *sang.* Is that true?

A: [Laughs.] Isn't that funny? No, the singing was in labor.

S: Oh!

A: I remember being in the labor room and the pains were coming and nobody was doin' anything, so I started *singing.*

S: What did you sing?

A: It seems to me I was singing melodies I didn't even know [S laughs]. Beethoven [S laughs] and musical comedy maybe. Anything, just to pass the time [both laugh together]. That's a funny thing to remember.

About the date of her birth: June 4th was a *terribly* hot day, and in the hospitals at that time they put you on rubber sheets. Couldn't have been worse [A laughs, then S joins in]. They don't treat you that way anymore [both still laughing] at the hospital.

The only other time you and I spent the night together in the hospital was just before you died when they moved out the person in the bed next to yours, and David and I were invited to sleep there the night we arrived because the nurse thought it would be your last. It wasn't, and the next day when you were in a coma I described that room to you, with its wide windows and its pretty pastel walls and its view of the sky and its non-rubber sheets.

But nobody sang, and it isn't a funny thing to remember.

Susan: So you found that you were able to work full-time and enjoy motherhood?

Alice: Oh yes. *No* question in my mind. At no time did I *not* like motherhood. I always was proud of my children and loved them terribly much.

S: That's what I've heard.

A: And my husband did, *too.* We both loved the children, and they were Number One in our lives. As a matter of fact, I don't remember going out in an evening more than two or three times. . . . I did belong to a co-op where neighbors would watch our children and then we would watch theirs. And I didn't take advantage of it much. I felt . . . special. . . .

The rest of your sentence is inaudible, covered over by my question: "Was this when your children were in elementary school?" (to which you answer, "Yes").

Alice: We never went anywhere without the children, all of their junior lives [A laughs at her own phrase]. We took trips, always with the kids.

And I give my husband credit for *this:* he would figure out places to go. Every single week, it seemed to me, we would do something with the children, every Saturday or Sunday. We would just pack lunches and get in the car and *go.* And I can't think of *why* [pause] I would ever want to plan a social event without them. I know I never did.

Susan: Did you have friends with children the same age as yours /A: Yes/ so that you could see other women, for example, socially, while your children played together?

A: Yes, but I didn't do too much of that. I was busy in the house, washing clothes or fixing dinner or something. There wasn't that much *time.* I evidently was never too socially inclined. I didn't need *that*. I didn't need the women and their lunches, or gossip over the fence, or anything. I never missed it, I never wanted it, I never thought of it.

Perhaps I expected a different version of your social life as a young mother, and I am forcefully answered. I hear your emphasis on the lack of leisure that characterized your own growing up and on work to be done. And now I hear something else: a refusal to be one of the "ladies who lunch," a refusal that informed your whole life.

I ask about the birth of your second child in the fall of 1943.

Alice: World War II was on in full force. . . . The night he was to be born, he came rather quickly. Very nice of him to do that, but we called the doctor and there were no vacant hospital beds to be had. My mother and father were visiting, getting ready to stay with the older child while I went to the hospital, but when this baby started coming fast and furious, we called my mother who had been a midwife in Europe and she came.

As I remember, the only thing she insisted on was that all the newspapers in the house be put under me, and a sheet on top of that. Then she just sat there, and I said, "Don't you *do* anything, Mom?" [S begins to laugh]. "Aren't you supposed to do something?" and she said, "No" [S laughing]. She said [S still laughing; A laughs] it's a cardinal principle in midwifery to let the baby come *naturally* [the sound of this word has a particularly lovely musical quality] and the midwife *knows* when there is a problem and it's her job to call a doctor if anything goes wrong. Basically, the baby is supposed to come naturally. She did the little things that were necessary. Of course, the father of the baby was very jumpy and itchy, and to calm him down I remember her sending him in to boil water [both laugh].

Susan: Did she use the water he boiled?

A: I think she *may* have used it to scald scissors or a knife to cut the cord. . . . He felt important; he had something to do. But, basically, she was the one standing by, and evidently nothing had to be done.

"She was the one standing by": your mother appears at the edges of your life, a woman so calm in crises, so shadowy in our memories. Under her gaze, you give birth to my brother.

I ask how you lost the woman who had provided child care while you worked.

Alice: She left to go to the Campbell Soup Company in Philadelphia because she was going to get a lot of money. They were dying for help; all the men were going off to war. So she just went. I tried to get another good maid, and then I decided now this makes no sense. I don't like uprooting children or disturbing their sense of [pause] order. The new maid might not be good, and I'd have to try someone else. I thought, no, I guess this is the time for *me* to stay home. The war effort [A laughs] requires me to be here rather than working for the government [longer pause].

So I, I resigned at that point and did not go back. [Wistful tone] And, you might ask, did I miss it? Well, I think I *did* for a while because I enjoyed the companionship of working women [pause].

And I pause, thinking of what you missed.
At my instigation, you discuss your daughter's tree-climbing skills.

Alice: Susan was such an active little thing that at about age three and a half, she'd be out in the backyard where there were many apple trees, which are wonderful for climbing because they've low branches . . . I didn't watch her all the time. I did have a good

Mother and Son: Alice and Kenneth Letzler. Orchard Beach, New York, August 1945.

Kenneth Letzler. Daytona Beach, Florida, 1950.

view from the kitchen window and I *would* check on her constantly. A little boy who was visiting would play with the children, who were somewhat younger than he, and at one point he characterized Susan as "the tree-climbingest young'un ah ever did see" [strong happy voice; both laugh]. I remember that distinctly, and I won't forget she climbed trees because of it [both laugh].

How many of "my" early memories come to me by your watching and passing on to me what you watched? I remember the apple tree—I rescued somebody's kite from its leaves—I can even feel the branches scraping my hand and knees, but I see myself from that window where I never was. The maternal gaze returns as my own.

Susan: Can you remember your earliest active involvement in community life?

Alice: I remember walking, pushing a baby carriage, when we were fighting for better schools. We had a mothers' march, a very informal sort of thing where we'd go around the block [both laugh]. I remember wheeling the baby carriage and Susan perhaps riding a little tricycle behind me with some kind of a poster [both laugh]. She got involved quite quickly, too. She was delighted. A lot of the children were walking along with their mothers. So that must have been one of the first things. [S has no memory of this at all.]

I got involved in what we called Fight for Better Schools because at the time our schools in Arlington were not very good. The superintendent of schools had been there for many, many years and he was a [pause] calamity. And we were determined to get rid of him before our kids went to school [both laugh]. Then a neighbor got me involved in the League of Women Voters. At the time, it was purely an educational organization. We didn't do lobbying, and I enjoyed it no end.

Susan and Alice Looking at Themselves Looking at Themselves.
Arlington, Virginia, January 1941.

*I notice how often the word "enjoyed" appears in your narrative. It was
there in your story of buying Christmas merchandise for your father's Brooklyn store. Joy—and pride—in the work you do accompany all the projects of
your life.*

Alice: It [the League] was a group which taught most of us to become good discussion participants *and* leaders. I give it a great deal of credit for giving me the knowledge of the fact that I *could* lead discussions. So I was in great demand many, many times in future years to do that. Really enjoyed it.

Then PTA was the next big thing that came in my life, and that was when Susan started school. Grade 1! [voice vigorous; S laughs]. From that time on, I was *never* out of PTA as long as my children were in elementary and high school. I did give a great deal of time and effort to it, and I enjoyed it, partly probably because I had been a teacher and was interested in education.

One year I even succumbed and let them put me up for president. The next year I was a vice president and then chairman of Parent Education, during which time I would write pamphlets all the time.

Susan: Oh?

A: I have copies of them, little booklets saying how to have a good teacher-parent conference, for example /S: Hmm/, and other booklets.

I look now at one of these booklets, prepared for the Arlington County Public Schools and entitled "Parents' Guide to Successful Conferences." In it you write, "In a good parent-teacher conference there is opportunity for each to ask questions of the other." [5] You encourage parent and teacher to be "open-minded" and to bring to each conference "a sincere respect for the other's unique knowledge of certain aspects of the child's behavior." None of this surprises me. Then I notice something else: "Both parents should try to attend the conferences. The father has just as much interest in . . . talking things over with his child's teacher as the mother has." A summary of questionnaires returned during the 1951–52 school year shows that 5,844 mothers and 391 fathers attended parent-teacher conferences. I'm sure Dad was one of them.

Alice: I was on the state board of the PTA for ten years in many, many positions—you had to be chairman of a committee to be on the board—and then finally I was *elected* state secretary. And I *did* really enjoy those years.

"Armor's Undermining Modesty" is the title Marianne Moore gives to her poem about certain knights who "did not let self bar / their usefulness to others who were / different." [6] *There is an undermining modesty in your whole life. And it gives me unexpected pleasure to hear you talk so openly and fully, for once, about your own quests and feats. "Self" did not bar your "usefulness to others who were / different."*

Alice: We would go down to board meetings, two to four times a year, in Richmond, Lynchburg, or Roanoke. One year we tried to have them in Northern Virginia. . . . That was a disaster. They never again came back to Northern Virginia for one of our big state conventions because it was too expensive for most people and we had to learn it the hard way [sighs]. . . . So for the rest of the time we mostly alternated between Richmond and Roanoke. And I enjoyed that very much.

Finally, I had to say, "Ten years is enough." They argued with me at first, but I thought, "No, it's time to move on." And that's when I left.

Before you left teaching, you consulted with your principal who said, "You go," and you did. Now you consult with colleagues who tell you to stay and you go. But, for you, moving on does not mean abandoning what you leave.

You hold "life membership" in what you have loved.

Alice: But I still have an honorary life membership in the PTA.

Susan: Oh, I didn't know that.

A: Oh yes. I carry it around with me somewhere [laughs softly].

I ask about the large brass school bell that once had pride of place on the mantel and now rests on a low table next to your sickbed in the room where we sit, its new function heartbreakingly evident.

Alice: The teachers in Arlington County one year decided that they would like to honor a layperson who had done a great deal for the schools: I was granted the first School Bell Award. It was partly based on my taking over the project of finding housing for teachers. I did it without pay. And it was quite a chore. . . .

Rereading my transcript, I notice how you focus on providing what people can afford: decent housing for college graduates and young parents; state conventions that are within the means of all delegates; accommodations for new teachers with limited incomes.

I ask about other fights you fought in Virginia.

Susan: Were there also political issues that . . .

Alice: We had to fight politics to get what we think was necessary. We fought for an *elected* school board [strong vigorous voice] and we *got* it. But shortly after we got it, we lost the right to have a school board elected *because* it was the time of desegregation: we were fighting up here to have our schools integrated, and they were fighting down in Richmond to hold the line with massive resistance

The First School Bell Award.
Arlington, Virginia, May 15, 1962.

[pause; a small sigh]. [In Virginia, a "state law passed in 1956 known as 'massive resistance,' . . . created a voucher program to allow white children to attend private schools."][7]

I ask how you became involved with the Northern Virginia Opera and the Arlington-based International Folk Festival.

Alice: That was later on, when . . . the nest was empty. I succumbed to suggestions that I go to these other groups, and I did. . . . As you can see, I did let fate lead me where I had to go. I didn't hesitate too long when opportunity knocked and I went my way. But I hardly ever went out seeking these things, as you can see.

What do I see? A receptivity to circumstances ("I did let fate lead me.
. . . I hardly ever went out seeking . . .") and a readiness to respond to a
call ("I didn't hesitate too long . . ."), but also a kind of covert self-assertion
("I went my way . . ."). It is a matter of continually shifting emphasis: fate
led, but you went your way. A complicated sense of "fate," perhaps something
like that inscribed in the classical texts you studied, connects you with the
events of your own life.

The Northern Virginia Folk Festival was a gigantic, biennial, multina-
tional event that featured the culture, traditions, and culinary and artistic tal-
ents of many hundreds of people in Northern Virginia, Maryland, and
Washington, D.C. At the Department of Parks, Recreation, and Commu-
nity Resources, you and its first coordinator, Priscilla Urner, "worked up this
folk festival and it's still going on."

Alice: After a while when Priscilla left, I was supposed to take
over, but again I did not want the top job. I never wanted to feel
pinned down. I had, supposedly, a part-time job which had in-
creased in hours each week. Nobody really knew how much time I
put in. I worked on it very hard *and* enjoyed it, and did well working with the foreign nationals who performed at the folk festival,
but I still maintained that I would be the *assistant* to the coordinator
who would deal with money, the budget, funding.

Susan: I know something of the success of the folk festival over
the years, and I know that in many ways you would run things behind the scenes. I imagine you don't care to comment on why you
wouldn't want to step into the first position and be *seen* as having the
full responsibility?

A: I really don't know how to answer it. You noticed we talked
about it a number of times, where I finally would yield and become
president of the class, for instance, and then I would step back again.
I never enjoyed the top job where you are totally visible and to-

tally—I was going to say totally accountable for your actions, but I never did anything for which I didn't want to be accountable. I didn't want to have to deal with those top decisions while there were so many underlying important things to be done. I rather wanted to be in the *doing* part of it than in the final decision making.

I remember your saying long ago that whenever you saw a work crew, there was always one person doing nothing, and that was the one in charge.

Alice: [Pause.] But, you see, people would perceive that I was very capable of a top job and so occasionally they would push me into it, but I would pull back as soon as I could. I don't know how else to explain it . . . [laughs ruefully]. Whenever I took the top job I would work so hard at it, it would be more than the job warranted, in a way. I remember when I was president of PTA at [Kate Waller] Barrett School, I liked the prestige, I should *think* I did, but I always felt I wanted to be *doing* more. This way I felt you had to delegate: let other people do these jobs. Sometimes they didn't do them as well as I would have liked to see them done. Perhaps that's what bothered me.

What I mean is things just *build* when I get my fingers in them. I remember when Mr. Rignall, the principal, whom I was very fond of, left to take a job in South America. Before we knew it [strong voice returns], we had a whole crew of people writing a play [voice becoming stronger] in his honor. I can remember them sitting around that dining room table [pointing to it]. We had a *marvelous* time writing it. And then we had to cast it; then we had to rehearse it. And everything got so *big* [A laughs; pause].

While I was in college, you served for three years as chairman of the Arlington County School Board's twenty-one-member Advisory Council

on Curriculum. In one of the speeches you gave at that time, you argue for the possibility of real change: "There is great satisfaction in working on these [curriculum] task groups. One learns a great deal in the process. Looking at it from a community point of view, I would say the greatest value of this continuing participation in school matters is that we are doing something here to counteract the complacency that sets in when we think we have achieved excellent schools."[8] You claim to be representing a community point of view. It would be wonderful if you were. But more wonderful to me is that you are clearly "looking at it" from a point of view of your own, one that I now share.

I ask what turns out to be my last question. It has to do with trips and journeys. First, you mention visits to Florida, where both your parents are buried: winter vacations that ended when my father died.

Alice: I have a number of friends in Florida who keep asking me to come back, but I haven't gone back since our last visit together [sad voice; a very long pause].

Then you tell me about your two "once-in-a-lifetime trips." The first was a thirty-day family vacation in the summer of 1952 when we drove across the country, camping in our green tent every night but two. Your voice sparkles.

Alice: I just loved it because I was outdoors, staying in state or national or local parks [voice happy, vibrant], seeing nature and seeing the country: the Grand Canyon, Yellowstone, Mesa Verde, Grand Tetons. I loved it, no doubt about it. . . .

Now, the other trip, Dad and I went alone. He had been wanting me to take trips, and I somehow fought them off. But this time he had arranged for us to take a Caribbean cruise without consulting me.

Susan: Oh?

A: Because he was afraid I'd turn everything down.

S: Oh.

A: And he went all out. He got one of the best cabins you could get to make sure that I wouldn't get seasick and wouldn't regret going. And it was a *wonderful* trip. We went on a ship called the *Song of Norway*, a white gleaming ship. It left from Miami and spent seven days in the Caribbean, stopping at several of the little islands /S: Mmm/. That trip was just delightful [richly happy voice; S laughs]. There was an awful lot of food. . . . At first you thought you had to eat everything [S laughs] because cruises *do* provide you with luxuries you never dream of [happy, mischievous voice; S laughs]. . . .

One of the pleasures of that trip on the water was to watch the sunset. And so, actually, we had to change our dinner time. We took the late seating just so I could see the sun go down, because the sun goes down very fast and that interfered with the first seating. And we'd *race* out there at whatever time the sun was to set that day [S is laughing; laughter and a crescendo of excitement in A's voice], and that's the way we liked it. We would stand there and watch that red sun come down [voice speeding up]. It would go down, down, down [musical, vibrant voice], as far as you could see, touching the water—and then it would *drop* over the horizon, it would drop . . . in ten seconds it'd be gone.

But it was the most beautiful sight [S laughs], and then we'd walk around the deck for a while, and then it was time for the second seating . . . [*Click*].

Our conversation seems finished; then there is an epilogue:

Susan: I hope my laughter doesn't seem excessive, but there is a delight in *watching* this narration that may not be accessible to someone simply listening to the tape recording [pause], so . . . [*Click*].

It is finished. Then I hear our two voices one last time:

Susan: This is really quite a workout, isn't it?
Alice: *Digging* into my memory? Yes.

The sun goes down, you and Dad go on to "the late seating," the recorder clicks off. A voice delivers an epilogue. There is another click, but this is not the end. There is one more antiphonal exchange. The final image is of digging, digging into what is buried in memory.

Listening to, and transcribing, these tapes has become my necessary ritual of mourning, my performance of ambivalence, our double rite of passage. It is an unburying of the maternal voice, a voice that becomes a text, however incompletely inscribed, whose reader will no longer gaze at the space left by your silence.

Always you seem to sense ahead of anyone else when you are to "move on."

PART 3

Summer 1926
& Summer 1996

Life can only be lived forward and understood backward.
—Søren Kierkegaard

September 9, 1994

Dear Alice,

I have been looking through the gray metal file cabinet in which my brother placed the documents and papers you and Dad saved over the last seventy years. There—among old photographs and death certificates, canceled checks and newspaper clippings, an impressive translation of Horace (book 3, ode 9) made when you were seventeen, speeches and publications, copies of letters sent and letters received, your children's wedding invitations and your own honeymoon menus, citations for exemplary service to county and state—I found a diary you wrote in 1926. It begins the first day of summer vacation and ends suddenly on September 9, perhaps when school starts. You are fourteen years old: this is your first, and possibly your only, diary. It is marked "Private." You are not here to tell me not to read it. I don't know what you would say to me if you were to have a hand in deciding what to do. I wait an hour. This time I open your "box of letters."

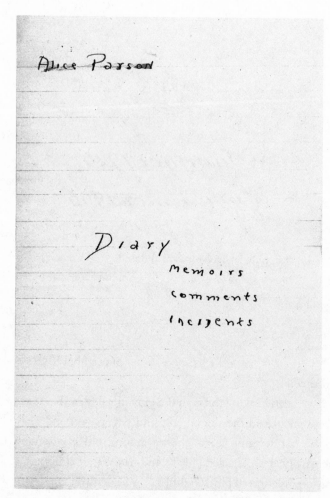

Alice Parson's Diary: Title Page.

Alice Parson

Diary

July 1, 1926   Thursday

At last I've really started to write entries in a diary!

This is the first day of my summer vacation after the completion of my second year at Erasmus High.

Today, I cleaned up in the house a bit, and then stayed in

Alice Parson's Diary: First Page.

the store, where I fixed up the novelty case for father and started helping make the bills. Uncle Ben's arrival interrupted this. I practiced [piano?] a while and then went out for a game with Will.

July 2nd, 1926   Friday

To-day, I got up early and helped papa in the store to

prove that 'I'm not in school!' After loafing and practicing, Will and I went to the Beverly to see Colleen Moore in 'Irene.'

July 3rd, 1926   Saturday

Vic and Bobby moved around here to-day and we went to see their rooms.

Summer 1996

Dear Alice Parson,

I have read the diary written in your fourteenth summer. You begin on July 1, 1926, in a voice filled with exhilaration. It is your first day as a diarist: "At last I've really started to write entries in a diary!"

How you must have looked forward to a holiday of writing days!

During the first week of your vacation, you clean the house, write bills, practice the piano, help your father in the candy store, see a movie with your brother, go on an outing "in Mr. Lapidus' soft-easy-going car," and miss the fun of July 4th fireworks. ("The famous 4th falls on the 5th this year," you write, "because the 4th is Sunday.") On July 6, your mother won't let you go to the dentist in the Bronx because of a subway strike on the I.R.T. "But that was all right 'by me.' "The next day you do "nothing but read a whole book and half a magazine—in bed." The wonder lies in giving yourself to nothing but your own pleasure, all day.

At the end of your entry on July 8, you quietly note: "Looks like mama doesn't feel well. She went to the beach and came back not feeling any better." And thus begins a summer of writing in the face of your mother's absence, a summer like my own summers now, writing in the absence of the mother you became.

On July 9 you report, "Mama was in bed, so I had to do duty in house and store all day." Your diary becomes a record of your reti-

cences. "Ordinary" life continues, its ordinariness achieved by shifting self-pity and rebellion to the margins. The undiagnosed illness of
your mother remains in the background, attended in its fluctuations
not by medical supervision but by a daughter's bewilderment:

> Aug 2nd   Monday
>
> Mama doesn't feel so good to-day. *(Well* somehow
> doesn't seem right there. Why?) But I'm hoping it's just the
> "not so good" she had before the "very good." In other
> words, maybe she's getting rid of the phlegm and to-mor-
> row'll be well.

As you try to understand your mother's sickness, you pause to question your own writing. Your attention to language is itself a way of
confronting slippage and loss. In writing to yourself, you rephrase
("In other words . . ."), telling the tale again, more hopefully: "and
to-morrow'll be well."

Your diary is your "letters to Alice," written when other letters
go unanswered.

> Friday   Sept. 3rd
>
> I wonder why Rose doesn't write to me. It's very unusual
> and I don't like it. I received *my* letter back, wrong address.
> Before Rose went away, she gave me the address, but it evi-
> dently wasn't quite right.

I understand what you feel, Alice. I write you at fourteen; I wrote
you after your death. I too receive my letters back. But it's not
"unusual."

During the summer of her illness, you attempt to mother your
mother and fail in small ways that loom large; your diary records the
tears you hide from others. On Saturday, July 10, in unbearable summer heat, you try to make salmon cutlets for dinner: "It looks so

easy. . . . It started off fine, but ended up in crumbs. Immediately I began to be a gusher but it was stupid." The daughter's tears gush, but the diarist rescues the moment by entering, rather than dismissing, it:

> It wasn't so bad anyway, because the crumbs were good and crisp and the hot corn was soft and good.

The sensuous images, and the repetition of "good" in a near-chiasmus (a word you may have learned in Latin class), transform an anticipated loss into an unexpected pleasure. It is a small but important triumph: you write yourself into and out of girlishness in the absence of your mother.

Unthinkable loss is the unwritable text, isn't it, Alice? When on the next day your Aunt Mary shows you how to make a noodle pudding, you write, half-facetiously:

> I pity myself, when mama gets up. She [will] try to teach me how to make e<u>very</u> bl<u>ess</u>ed thing.

The "pity" is that mama does not, might not, get up. The half-underlined words, "every" and "blessed," show the half-heartedness of your jokey complaint. But what gives you away is the uncharacteristic omission of "will" after "She." When the subject of the sentence is your mother, you leave out the future tense. Your next sentence is more straightforward: "But I need to learn, so that's alright, or let's hope it will be *all* right." I know you are learning more than how to make a noodle pudding.

In the summer of 1926, you write of free passes to movies, fireworks you never see, putting on a play, persistent rain and dreary days, New York beaches, newspaper routes, chicken soup and noodle pudding, Uncle Harry's automobile accident; you write about unanswered letters, friendlessness in Brooklyn, your mother's mysterious illness, and a new blue raincoat you never got. Your sturdy farewell to that raincoat ("Goodbye Slicker! Fate.") is one of the more poignant moments in your diary. The slicker is one of the few "luxuries" you allow yourself to yearn for. And yet, Alice, you accept "Fate."

Where fun can be found, you find it—at the movies, in the ocean with water wings (you don't know how to swim), playing solitaire by yourself and checkers with Bill, eating Fig Newtons and jelly apples at Coney Island with your friend Rose, being treated by Hanalaki (who is Hanalaki?) to an ice cream soda in Manhattan, riding to Coney Island in Uncle Harry's "dandy" new Nash, and taking a momentous family boat trip to Bear Mountain on the *De Witt Clinton* during a heavy downpour. When the neighborhood children decide to put on a play with "local talent," you are asked to be assistant director, and you write in your diary on July 15: "I have an awfully funny feeling about this business because I feel so kiddish." Then you add: "I'm not taken at my right value." The words leap out at me:

I'm not taken at my right value.

At fourteen, in the midst of an extraordinary motherless summer—when you have folded yourself into the needs of your family—you casually affirm your "right value" with utter self-confidence. And this is the Alice I know, though not many others did: the dutiful, self-denying, modest woman I knew always knew her right value, even when she most seemed not to.

It is the most intimate moment in your diary, your most private and hidden avowal. It is the Alice I miss.

June 1, 1996

Dear Alice Parson,

"Helpful and kind, with no fantastic fribbles." This quote (from *Faust*) will appear under your name in the 1932 Hunter College yearbook when you are a senior. The description beneath the quote says that "Alice, modestly reticent as to her private life, has to be prompted for information." Why am I not surprised? All that can be discovered in an interview with Alice Parson is that she likes moonlight, spring, a roadster, and the legitimate stage. "Do you like the movies?" she is asked.

"No, I don't care for the movies very much."

Now this is the Alice I knew, but I am not writing the Alice I knew. I am writing you, a kid who went to the movies every chance you got, who begins and ends your 1926 diary with the names of films you saw. I am writing you, Alice Parson, the mother who isn't there yet.

June 2, 1996

Dear Alice Parson,

Who are you?

You are not me at fourteen and you won't be me at thirty-one or at fifty-six.

I like the way you flick off self-blame on July 4: "William was angry tho', because I couldn't find him at the Parade Ground. So he couldn't go [to Sea Gate]. What's the difference? He went to Coney with Vic and Bob." I like that sudden flash of self-esteem on July 15: "I'm not taken at my right value." I'm impressed by your solution to the problem of how to cut up a chicken on Sunday, July 18: "William took one end and I took another and biff! . . . The thing was apart." I'm charmed by your story on July 20 of a one-legged Irish Catholic serenading the subway car to Coney Island. I'm delighted by the kid who flatly contradicts the dentist in the Bronx on August 4: "[He] says one of my teeth is in very bad condition, and doesn't want to believe that hot or cold water doesn't hurt it. It doesn't." I'm intrigued that you read a story written by another Alice, a story with the potentially irreverent title, *Are Parents People?* I'm startled by your sudden, uninhibited self-lament on July 25:

"Pretty soon Will and I'll forget we ever saw movies. Another Sunday has passed. Terrible! Terrible!"

You at fourteen are a surprise.

June 3, 1996

Dear Alice Parson,

There are so many names I've never heard before in your diary: Vic and Bobby, Sophie, Welton, Spinach, the ever-present Fannie, Lillian, Mrs. Kaplan, Lennie, Ruth, Stanley, Mr. Lapidus, the Sickle kids. And there are so many uncles and aunts I never met: Uncle Ben, Uncle Dave, Uncle Harry with his various cars, Aunt Sarah, Aunt Katie, Aunt Mary, Aunt Julie. And yet how very lonely you sound, Alice Parson. On July 15, you write: "I wish Rose lived here. There isn't a girl I could call my *friend* around here."

What do you do? You go to the movies: *Irene; Tramp! Tramp! Tramp!* ("good and funny"); *The Wilderness Woman* ("Funny. Good acting."); *Buowa Derby;* and *Laff That Off* ("a comedy mixed with pathos"). You see the dentist in the Bronx irregularly and dispiritedly; you iron, cook, help with the store and the paper route. With relatives you make excursions to Coney Island, Manhattan Beach, Brighton Beach, Sea Gate, and Bear Mountain. You walk to the library, the book store, the post office; you buy black shoes, write three letters (one in French), visit the automat and the *New Leader* office, and become assistant director of a neighborhood play.

You read eleven books in July 1926, each carefully noted at the back of your diary: *Home Maker,* by Dorothy Canfield; *The Flirt,* by Booth Tarkington; *Oh. Money! Money!,* by Eleanor H. Porter; *The Black Company,* by W. M. B. Ferguson; *Are Parents People?,* by Alice Duer Miller; *Last Bow,* by Conan Doyle; *Daughter of the House,* by Carolyn Wells; *Miranda,* by Margaret L. H. Lutz; *Face Cards,* by Carolyn Wells; *Tides of Barnegat* (no author listed); *The White Flag,* by Gene Stratton-Porter.

I look in frustration at these eleven titles. I have read none of them. Why and how did you choose them? Unlike the movies, which you do not hesitate to evaluate, these books are never discussed in your diary. Certain titles, *Daughter of the House* and *Home Maker,* characterize your life this summer, but this is hardly true of *The Flirt.* Though I am eventually a product of it, your sexual life remains hidden.

Ocean is the great site of pleasure in your diary. You delight in the summer sky and in the "dandy" waves that "just picked you up." After a visit to Coney Island on a hot July day, you write:

> I can really swim with wings and I had confidence enough to make 3 strokes without them! What do you think of that?

What do I think of that? That is how I see you: with a little assistance, you navigate the ebb and flow of the summer of 1926.

June 4, 1996

Dear Alice Parson,

You talk about your mother's tears on Sunday, August 1.

> It's August. A whole month is gone and still Mama's in bed. I don't know what to think. She's so weakened up that the sight of Mrs. Perlberg and an old friend of theirs made her cry. She was well again a little later.

I too don't know what to think. Again and again, your mother seems better, then relapses. On Wednesday, July 28, you had written: "Mama's really sick this time. It's almost 3 weeks. We at last called the doctor. He gave her an injection [of what?] to bring relief. Mama felt a little better at night." Does your mama, weeping at the sight of Mrs. Perlberg and an old friend, think she may die? Do you?

Finally, on August 19, you write: "These days mama is almost entirely well again. She makes dinner and the [newspaper] route, tho' I still get up early to give papa breakfast." Beneath your careful reporting of the stages of her illness, was there terror?

June 5, 1996

Dear Alice Parson,

You, a young girl without a room of her own, are keeping a diary. Where can it be hidden? How safe can it be? How can it reveal the secrets of someone "modestly reticent as to her private life"? What can it prompt? Like the photographs I have of you and your mother, it is a gesture in the direction of what it conceals.

My heart goes out to you, Alice Parson, barely fourteen, unmothered for almost a whole summer.

As I begin my sixth motherless summer, what can I say to you? How can I tell you what it's like to lose the mother you became? I wrote letters to her. I listened to her voice. I came to the end of my resources. Then I found a trove of words I didn't know existed—but they are your words, Alice Parson, not my mother's. And so my dialogue continues with another Alice.

We are a woman and a young girl, dealing with the loss of a maternal presence. You do not acknowledge the possibility of your mother's death; my letters to my mother after her death are, by their very existence, a profound denial of absolute loss. You call your daily recordings a diary; I call mine echolocations. You write, one summer in the '20s, to yourself; now I write, seventy summers later, to you.

You write before the loss: I write the loss.

June 6, 1996

Dear Alice Parson,

I am reading your diary again today. I thought I would feel joy in the simple act of rereading what had come to an end.

For a moment you rise up, quite alive, in your excited opening sentence. Then I am alone, my solitude merely deepened by my return as reader to what the writer has left behind.

June 7, 1996

Dear Alice Parson,

Somewhere beyond the silence of so much unrecorded life you existed. In the opaqueness of your diary you prefigure the woman I knew, and that opaqueness inspires all I write.

Again I send letters that will never be answered.

June 10, 1996

Dear Alice Parson,

I probably shouldn't tell you this, but for several days I have thought I would not write you any more. I didn't like myself at fourteen; girls that age generally give me the willies. Why don't I ditch you?

You are someone I have never met. We are crossing shadows.

In the evening I wonder if I will have anything to say to you when I wake the next day.

Why don't I ditch you?

June 11, 1996

Dear Alice Parson,

I finally sent a draft of the first two parts of *Missing Alice* to your brother "Will" (a name I never heard him called). Uncle Bill replies within a week, having read the manuscript through "at a single sitting, directly on arrival":

> Your book is written, so I hesitate to bring up the tumble of questions coming to my mind, and I would suppose to

Alice! There was a pervasive family lack of personal inquiry and discussion. For example, I was *never* told by my parents that Rudy was a half-brother. The veil over life before coming to America was in essence never opened. Did Alice attempt to penetrate it? I never did, and why not? Did anyone attempt to "understand" our mother's disintegration, loss of self-esteem, and chronic debilitating asthma? Years later there was a miraculous response to management by visits to the Park Ave. office of Dr. A. Baruch, the senior chest physician at P. and S.

Why did our self-sacrificing idealistic "brilliant" father—committed to the Americanization and educational advancement of his children—never leave the role of shopkeeper? And was he "blind" to the social blunting of Alice's sleeping on a folding cot in the dining room?

All this and much more keep atumbling. So you see what you've done! Incidentally, I knew Leon well—the laundry man's older son. He, his younger brother and I sang from "Grand Opera at Home" at our piano. Alice is absent from those memories. I think her second suitor [whom she married] was a much better choice.[1]

Several times in the past three years, I had asked Bill to share his memories of your childhood and young girlhood. Always I received the same sad answer—there were none. In this letter he recalls Leon, his sister's first "suitor," but "Alice is absent from those memories."

Yet for me, as for Bill, the questions "keep atumbling." Did you, Alice, experience the social "blunting" your brother speaks of? Was your character dulled or sharpened by the circumstances of your adolescence? Is there a connection between your mother's emotional withdrawal and her "chronic debilitating asthma"? Who in your family was the person least "blind" to your deepest needs? Was it your papa, after all? And why does your brother's veil conceal all memories of you? What would you say to this "tumble of questions," Alice?

June 12, 1996

Dear Alice Parson,

In the envelope that contains Bill's letter is a separate letter from his wife, Buffy:

> [I] never had a daughter and always wanted one in order to find out if mothers and daughters can be real friends: You've answered my question, although I feel that you have succeeded only partially in opening Alice's great sense of privacy and reserve, which always perplexed me. After reading your touching story, I now wonder if I might have done more to elicit her confidence.[2]

I don't think it is merely a question of eliciting confidence. A life can be lived directly, yet not be told directly. I think that is what your diary tells us, Alice.

June 13, 1996

Dear Alice Parson,

The "story" I write seems to attract texts: letters, tapes, a diary; letters about letters, tapes, and a diary; speeches, committee reports, telegrams, "little booklets," death certificates; memoirs and memories collide, collaborate.

Buffy says in her letter that she is trying to write her "own story—mainly for myself, to refresh my memory. . . . I said to Bill: 'Tell me about your father,' before I had met him. Bill's answer was that he was like Jesus: And he meant it."

In *Missing Alice,* I praise the parent you will become in terms that must sound suspiciously inflated. Even your brother will tell me: "You offer barely a clue as to the factors that may contribute to your own devoted sanctification of Alice."[3] (This from a man who compared a parent to Jesus!) Are there really no clues? Like your father, my mother had a warmth that never abated, a lack of stinginess, truly astonishing kindness coupled with an absence of pretensions, remarkable intelligence, and extraordinary gifts of the heart.

Can it be, Alice, that after all these years you are still invisible, even to your kid brother?

June 14, 1996

Dear Alice Parson,

Now I cannot stop writing you and I cannot write letters to anyone else. I pack up what I have written and hide it away. I walk out of the room, but your diary calls after me. *You aren't through with me!* it cries.

June 16, 1996
New York City

Dear Alice Parson,

When I wrote my mother after her death, I dreamed of her often. I dreamed of her not always as I had known her: she would appear wearing clothes she never wore, saying things she'd never said, doing things she had never done. Once in my dreams my mother marries a young, stocky, black-haired man who speaks Spanish and they have a child. If I can dream of my mother as a woman I never knew, why can't I dream of her as a girl I never met?

Why can't I dream of you, Alice?

June 17, 1996
New York City

Dear Alice Parson,

In a book I'm reading, *Aging and Its Discontents,* Kathleen Wood-ward suggests that the " 'essence' of a memory of someone [might] have to be that which we could *not* remember, never having known it."[4]

I write to you, Alice Parson, in order to remember what I never have known.

June 18, 1996

Dear Alice Parson,

Before me is an undated photograph of you smiling in a bathing suit, seated on the shoulders of another young smiling girl in a bathing suit. I don't know how old you are or who the other girl is, but I have decided that you are fourteen in this photo and this is the person I write to.

There are trees in the background and high grass in the foreground; no ocean, no sand. The other girl is wearing a bathing cap and your hair looks as if it's wet: you must have come from, or be near, water.

Wherever you are, it's summer, it's not a hot apartment in Brooklyn, and it's not "Terrible! Terrible!" I guess that's why I look at it as I write you this summer, Alice. *That* girl smiling in the photo could be someone I know, could even be me.

June 19, 1996

Dear Alice Parson,

I've been wondering if we could have been friends as adolescents. I found a list of forty-three books I read between June 16 and August 7, 1952. Apparently, I was competing for a library prize. On each page of a tiny booklet with "Books I Have Read" printed on its

Bathing, Not Swimming: Alice Parson (top) and friend.
New York, no date.

orange-brown cover, I am asked to note author, title, date begun and
finished, and "what I think of this book." Every page is stamped "Arlington County Library, Glencarlyn Branch." Next to each stamp
are the initials of various librarians: "L.M.F.," "P.B.," "M.M."; next to
each set of initials is a handwritten "o.k."

I am twelve years old, having just finished the sixth grade. At fourteen, in the summer of 1926, you have finished the tenth grade. Were it not for this required record of each book, I would know no more about my responses to my summer reading than I know about yours.

I read books on Wilbur and Orville Wright, spiders, Eskimos, the Old Testament David, New York, cowboys, the Canadian Mounties, the Trojan War, and animals, especially smart ones. I seem to have liked mysteries and ghost stories and biographies (James Fenimore Cooper, Clara Barton, Amelia Earhart, Lucretia Mott).

Here are my responses to three books by and about women:

Lucy Fitch Perkins, *The Spartan Twins,* begun and finished June 19, 1952: The ways in the middle of the 5th century B.C. certainly are different. They don't think women are anything!

Jane Moore Howe, *Amelia Earhart,* begun June 19 and finished June 20, 1952: Everybody said she couldn't do this and she couldn't do that because she was a girl. But she showed them when she flew the Atlantic Ocean.

Constance Buel Burnette, *Lucretia Mott,* begun July 3 and finished July 4, 1952: I think Lucretia was right in thinking that women should have as many privileges as men. Girls should be able to learn as much as boys too. I'm glad Lucretia fought for the rights of women.

You, in 1926, do not speak directly of sexism. I have only a possible hint of it after you are made *assistant* director of a play: "I'm not taken at my right value." You add, "Well, when among the Romans, do as they do in Rome or—just the opposite. But it means the same." And that's when you suddenly wish there was a girl close by whom you could call a friend.

Your father cannot afford to release you from the confusing

double roles of housewife-helpmate and adolescent daughter without a room of her own. You learn to be a Roman at home.

Would a girl you could have called your friend have shared your sense of your right value? I hope so. I do.

June 20, 1996

Dear Alice Parson,

I have just read the eleven-page diary I started when I was thirteen. It begins January 1, 1954, at the end of a winter vacation in Florida, and stops abruptly on January 11 when school is canceled due to a heavy snowfall ("will be 8 or 10 inches deep—swoon"). My diary mentions "handsome guys" in Miami; bringing home sixteen coconuts; feeling "silly standing outside at 10 degrees below, shivering . . . while my back is peeling & my nose has freckles on it." School begins and there are references to surprise tests in history, Eisenhower's State of the Union address on January 7, babysitting, gossiping in gym class, buying hose, popping popcorn, my broken clarinet, and a much-discussed "J.R.C. dance" on Friday night, January 8, with names of possible escorts blackened out: "I had fun by the tons, loads, & billions."

How different my girlhood was from yours.

June 21, 1996

Dear Alice Parson,

Yesterday it rained again.

Today is the first day of summer, the day when the light is supposed to last longest, but nobody notices because it is dreary and overcast. I remember your diary entry for August 20: "It looks as if the sun'll never shine again. If it doesn't rain, the day is dreary." The second sentence puzzled me until today, which was, in fact, "dreary" for lack of either sun *or* rain.

The woman who cuts my hair has just become a grandmother.

She has shortened her workweek by a day to babysit for her daughter's first child. As she was cutting my hair, Nancy said it was only when her daughter turned eighteen that they became friends. Before that there were too many "bumps and turns in the road."

One of the major bumps must be adolescence itself. My winter diary at thirteen is filled with talk about boys and dances, gossip and ecstasy at school's closing because of a snowstorm. My second eleven-page diary, written in July of 1955, recounts my summer life: I have long telephone conversations, swim, learn to jitterbug, picnic all day one day, see *I Love Melvin* (with Debbie Reynolds and Donald O'Connor), and meet someone named Tommy. At sixteen I finally keep a diary that lasts longer than eleven days. It begins on August 19 and ends November 12, 1956. The last eight pages, each dated and headed "Dear Diary," are left blank.

Which of my three adolescent diaries should I compare with yours? Shall I compare our journals as tenth graders? You are fourteen and I am sixteen. At that age, two years is an epoch.

I can't find a fit between our diaries.

The light of the longest day of the year has faded and for the first summer I can remember I didn't notice its passing.

June 22, 1996

Dear Alice Parson,

I am searching my tenth-grade diary for hints of something we might have in common. On August 23, 1956, my brother is at camp and my father is away on business in New York. My mother and I are alone, collecting and eating tomatoes from our garden "as fast as we can." I claim to be doing "all the cooking," which I list mockingly: "hot dogs, liver, hot dogs, eggs, hot dogs, soup, hot dogs, spagetti [*sic*], hot dogs, sandwiches, etc." I go with my mother to buy shoes for school, as you and Will did with your Aunt Mary. Then a casual note: "Mom got sick." I cancel a date for that evening. On August 24,

I mow the front and back lawn, wash the car, run around the block with my dog, Cocoa, and visit with friends. "Daddy came home 9:40 p.m.!" There is no more mention of home duties or sickness.

The following day there is a brief entry, the kind I do not find in your diary, Alice: "Had a fight with parents." That evening my "family went to Hot Shoppe [for dinner], then . . . to Capitol steps and heard Air Force Band's last concert." There are no family outings like this in your diary of life in Brooklyn.

On August 28, I confide that I am embarrassed when my mother, whom I have been urging to see some "halfway-decent" movies, accompanies my brother to the "Kiddie Show" at a local movie theater. On September 20, "Mom's pretty wonderful" because she's teaching an eleventh-grade homebound girl French, English, History, and Algebra I. I do not find these shifting responses to your mother in your diary, Alice; you seem neither embarrassed by nor proud of her.

On September 30, one of my friends drives my father to National Airport for his flight to New York because "Mom didn't feel up to it," but the next day she attends a hilarious "Donkey Basketball" game at my high school, in which all my teachers take part. But in your diary, Alice, I find no merriment shared with your mother.

The rest of my tenth-grade diary mainly records social activities: concerts, movies, slumber parties; baking cupcakes; borrowing and playing records; swimming, long walks, rides in friends' new cars, outdoor cookouts, county fairs. After school begins, there are pop quizzes, too much homework ("I hate Algebra II"), clarinet lessons, band practice, broken school buses, club meetings, school dances, athletic events, and more movies.

I saw *The Proud and the Profane, Bus Stop, War and Peace,* and *Giant,* with boys named Terry and John and Danny, never with girl-friends or my brother. You saw *Irene, Tramp! Tramp! Tramp!,* and *Laff*

That Off, with Lillian and Ruth and Fannie and with your brothers, Will and Rudy. I am sixteen and dating; you are fourteen and the boys you go out with are your relatives.

Tonight on the American Movie Channel I learn that over half the films made before 1950 no longer exist. Even the movies you saw are disappearing.

In the summer of 1956, my friends fill the house mornings, afternoons, evenings; they sleep in my room (I have a room of my own) and eat in our kitchen. My parents go out in the evenings, together and with their children. My brother and I do no work that adds to the family income; my mother's employment outside the home is usually unpaid. I swim whenever I like at a neighborhood pool two blocks from our house. My mother and father help me with my homework, attend school events, take their children on family vacations, have no serious or sustained illnesses during my childhood or adolescence.

But then I find an entry I had forgotten. On Monday, October 22, 1956, I write: "Mom's sick (flu?) & I drove to library and grocery store—alone—in the rain. First I couldn't get the car started—for 15 minutes I sat in the driveway, darn, darn, darn . . . Sylvia walked over with some troubles that were partly Julie's and partly Kathy's."

In both our diaries, an adolescent daughter falters at first, attempting to take on adult responsibilities in response to a mother's sudden illness. When your mother falls ill, the salmon cutlets you try to make "end up in crumbs." When I attempt to drive to the library and grocery store in the rain, I have trouble getting the car out of the driveway. You "gush" and I curse, but we do get on top of the situation. You deflect your frustration by focusing on something positive and sensuous: "It wasn't so bad anyway because the crumbs were good and crisp and the hot corn was soft and good." I deflect my sense of trouble by focusing on someone else's, or on someone who is focusing on someone else's: "Sylvia walked over with some troubles that were partly Julie's and partly

Kathy's." Both of us acknowledge obliquely the difficulty of a mother's undiagnosed illness. After your mother has been in bed for a month, you finally say, "I don't know what to think." I hide my anxiety by turning a diagnosis into a question, within a parenthesis: "(flu?)."

Could we have been friends, after all?

June 22, 1996

Dear Alice Parson,

In her eleven-poem sequence entitled "Domestic Interior," the Irish poet Eavan Boland writes: "There's a way of life / that is its own witness."[5]

That's how I think of you, Alice. And yet I seem to read your life more clearly when I read your diary against my own.

June 23, 1996

Dear Alice Parson,

After my mother's death I write (to paraphrase Sor Juana) into a silence that is filled with voices. The texts that I search for comfort are sites of absence. I write to the lost voice of nightly telephone conversations, and to the taped voice of a woman dying, and to the voice of a fourteen-year-old diarist, and even to the voice of my own adolescence.

I write in response to overheard remarks, casual questions, changes in weather, moonlight and night dreams and images that rise up before me as I awaken.

Would I not destroy all that I write in a minute, Alice, if I could hear for one moment the voice I seek?

Dear Alice Parson,

Looking for something else, I find a tiny Hallmark card. On the outside of the card there is a puppy wearing a red and blue plaid outfit. Inside there is a printed message telling me to

> Have a happy birthday
> With lots and lots of fun.
> Then have a happy year until
> You have another one!

It is signed, "Love—grandma Parson." I am startled. I don't remember ever seeing your mother's handwriting. It is more legible than mine but not so handsome as yours. There is a message written on the opposite page: "As I don't feel well and can not go out shopping, I am giving you $5 dollars for your birthday with best wishes. Many happy returns. Your mother will get you something nice. grandma."

I don't know what birthday this was; your mother died just after I was seven so this could be my fifth or sixth or seventh birthday. I don't remember the $5 or the "something nice" my mother must have bought me. I mostly remember your mother's being in bed, the other bed in my bedroom, with a never-identified illness. She was very weak but I don't remember tears, her daughter's or her own.

Finally, what went away was your mother, not her illness. I didn't see her dead or buried. It was my first experience of death and I never knew it.

The only written words I have from my grandmother, like the words you write about her, are from a time of illness. How odd. I wish I was making all this up.

June 24, 1996

Dear Alice Parson,

I have just come home from a mass for a dead colleague. It was a ceremony of great dignity and simple beauty, held in a carriage house converted to a chapel on the college campus. You and I don't write of death and its ceremonies in our diaries. I am not sure which parts of this experience to share with you.

The wife, father, and eldest son of my dead colleague remained outside the chapel to receive handshakes and hugs. The son, who was about seventeen, stood first in the greeting line. Very erect, in dark blue trousers, brown shoes, and a clean pressed white shirt open at the collar, he seemed the most poised of all of us. His face was a small, young version of his father's and he was without tears, unlike his mother and grandfather. I wondered if we were watching his courage or his incomprehension. This boy's father was hardworking, like yours and mine. Could you and I have stood this erect in the fading afternoon light if our fathers had dropped dead at the age of forty-three one ordinary Saturday in June?

The boy stood in the gray light that precedes rain and never wavered. The priest had said during the mass that the pain is with those left behind, not with the one who leaves, and that after we die, we will meet again those whom death has taken from us now. The first drops of rain begin to fall. The boy standing erect smiles after the last handshake.

June 24, 1996

Dear Alice Parson,

Three weeks ago one of my dearest colleagues, Florence Jacobson, professor of mathematics and "mother of us all," died at the age of seventy-eight, as you will. At the funeral, the rabbi said:

> It is a fearful thing
> to love
> what death can touch.

You are fourteen. Death hasn't touched you.

June 25, 1996

Dear Alice Parson,

I've been comparing your account of your mother's illness with my mother's recollection of it over sixty years later when she herself is terminally ill. The narratives are somewhat different in content and tone, and probably refer to two different periods of sickness. In the story my mother tells, the asthma is no longer mysterious. It is named and understood:

> I think I mentioned to you that in our family, as I recall, we had very little illness. And I don't remember [pause] taking pills. . . . Probably when I was twelve, after we moved to that Church Avenue address, I remember my mother had some severe asthma attacks and sometimes she had to go to bed, it was so bad . . . and I remember having her teach me from the bed [pause] how to make chicken dinner. . . . I remember I would go next door to Mr. Springer's [hearty voice] grocery and buy my vegetables and I guess I'd go down to Mr. Ring's butcher shop and get a chicken and she would tell me how to clean that chicken. . . . And I would have to singe the feathers off the chicken. We didn't cut it up. She taught me to make chicken soup with the chicken, so, actually, boiled chicken in soup is one of the first things I ever learned to make.

In your diary of 1926, there is no cooking lesson from a sick bed. There is no hearty voice of a shopper who buys vegetables from Mr. Springer and chicken from Mr. Ring. At fourteen, you are aided and instructed by aunts. Your attitude toward being taught by your mother is ambivalent: "I pity myself when mama gets up. She [will] try to teach me how to make every blessed thing. But I need to learn, so that's alright or let's hope it will be all right."

If the illness my mother remembers is of an earlier period, as she says ("[p]robably when I was twelve"), did you feel less threatened then by what had not yet become a pattern? Was taking on adult responsibilities at first exhilarating, less tiresome? Or do these two accounts simply reflect the difference between knowing and not knowing that your mother would be "almost entirely well again"?

These questions remain questions.

June 25, 1996

Dear Alice Parson,

Your comments about your father are so tender in your diary. I look again at the scattered sentences that create this impression:

> William and I gave papa a long-needed rest by closing the store for him [July 14].

> Hard luck Sunday for papa, alright!. . . . Therefore papa wakes his Allinku [a pet name for Alice] up at 7 [August 15].

> First of all, we unpacked the school supplies. That is, dad and I. . . . In the afternoon papa and I each took half and delivered Bill's paper route. . . .
>
> At night we put prices on the school bags and then—I was so knock[ed] out, I fell asleep without undressing, and papa got a laying out for letting me work so hard. Fate. Haint hit terrible! [August 17].

> In the evening papa and I gave the candies the good once-over—something they badly needed [August 25].

> Papa has a sort of case of hay fever. His eyes sting and his nose bothers [August 30].

In your diary, you and your father are often in synchronous movement: unpacking school supplies, making up prices, arranging shelves in the store, walking the paper route, bailing water out of the basement.

Your mother is often an isolated figure in her sickness, separated from the family:

> Mama was in bed, so I had to do duty in house and store all day [July 9].

> Mama didn't feel so well to-day. Most of the time I was in the store [July 13].

> Mama went out for a while to-day but she was very weak [July 24].

> A whole month is gone and still Mama's in bed. . . .
> Someone comes over almost every day now to help me [August 1 and 2].

> These days Mama is almost entirely well again. She makes dinner and the route, tho' I still get up early to give papa breakfast [August 19].

You and your father often appear in your sentences as a "we": "First of all, we unpacked. . . . In the afternoon papa and I. . . . in the evening papa and I." You take pleasure in working with him, in loving companionship. Even when "papa wakes his Allinku up at 7" (an event that would have been treated very differently in my diary), your sympathy is all with him: "Hard luck Sunday for papa. . . !"

You and your mother usually appear as separate subjects ("Mama was in bed, so I had to do duty in house and store all day"), in separate spaces ("Mama didn't feel so well to-day. Most of the time I was in the store"). She disappears from the sentence entirely the only time she is described in relationship to your father: "papa got a laying out for letting me work so hard."

Sixty-three years later you will say of your father: "He gave me any self-confidence I ever needed. . . . He had *complete* faith in me. . . . I think we had deep mutual love. . . . I felt his deep appreciation of me . . . and I hope he felt it in return." You will remember your mother as private and withdrawn, even when she is not ill: a "very dutiful" woman who lived a "quiet life." You do not know if she was happy: you never asked her questions.

Sixty-three years later you will tell me, "I guess I was a dutiful daughter." Yes, I think you were, Alice.

June 27, 1996

Dear Alice Parson,

Suddenly you are so close I can't see you any more.

June 28, 1996

Dear Alice Parson,

Today is my wedding anniversary.

Last night at 2 A.M. rain began to fall steadily. As I bent down to close the window, the smell of fresh night air was heart-stirring. I looked out over the back lawn and garages and saw the small lit tower on East Rock, whose spectacular cliff turns red in the twlight.

In your diary, you never speak of looking out windows. I know why: there was nothing to see. I try to remember the view from the upstairs back window on summer nights in Virginia when I was fourteen. There would have been a small square of closely cropped grass, and just beyond the grass roses, then corn, tomatoes, lettuce, and onions, and maybe some raspberries that had wandered in from the garden behind ours. Rising up in the far right corner near the chain-link fence would have been a mound of compost organized by my father. There were three trees, I think, two with bird feeders, and against the fence on one side, hydrangea and forsythia and, on the other, our small crape myrtle, a miracle of idiosyncratic bloom-ing. I could have smelled mint and honeysuckle, heard the mourn-ing doves, glimpsed lights flickering on or off in the upper floors of houses close by.

But now I remember: on summer nights when I was fourteen I didn't notice any of it.

June 29, 1996

Dear Alice Parson,

In the palm of my left hand, I hold your mother's vest-pocket Webster's Pronouncing Dictionary, bound in red leather faded and worn by frequent handling. The copyright is 1893 and the preface includes the following assertion by Alfred Ayres: "The manner in which one *speaks* his mother-tongue is looked upon as showing more clearly than any other one thing what his *culture* is and what his *associations* are and have been."[6] Where and with whom and when was your mother able to speak her culture, her education, her associations in her mother tongue? Is this tiny pronouncing diction-ary a clue to the mystery of your mother's hiddenness, her unwill-ingness or inability to expose herself in public? The only other possessions of hers I have inherited are a bulb-shaped piece of wood used in darning socks; three crochet hooks, two steel and one ivory; and a mysterious tortoiseshell cylinder with a knob at one end and a sharpened point at the other. When she gave me these a year before she died, my mother said one of them was valuable. I don't remem-ber which one and I don't crochet.

I hold the steel hooks in the palm of my left hand; they are ex-actly the same length as the vest-pocket Webster's. I stroke the rough leather surface of the tiny dictionary; the smoothness of the darning egg; the delicate, slender steel and the broken ivory base of the cro-chet hooks; the mysterious tortoiseshell. What do these objects tell me about my grandmother's life? More than I could have thought and less than I want to know.

June 30, 1996

Dear Alice Parson,

I will ask you a question I did not ask my mother: why do you not talk about the boys who must have been attracted to you? My adolescent diaries are not reticent about the attentions I received or responded to or discouraged. But I know nothing of your romantic life.

Only once, in a letter that arrives four years after the death of my mother, do I glimpse a young boy's response to her: "I first met [Alice] when she was a waitress at Camp Mt. Joy & I was a camper. She was about 18, possibly younger. I was about 13 or 14. Like many other lads, I fell in love with her."[7] The phrase, "Like many other lads," interests me. Where are these lads in your diary, in your memories? Do you not notice young boys' responses to you? Do you think that such responses are ephemeral, easily forgotten?

In a few years, a young boy will meet you and the impact of that experience will outlive you. Over sixty years later, he ends his letter to me: "The loveliness I saw in your mother when she was 18 stayed with her as it does with me now as I write you." You cannot possibly imagine such an event, can you, Alice? And, for all of your life, neither did I.

July 1, 1996

Dear Alice Parson,

It may surprise you to learn that I am reading Lewis Carroll's *Alice's Adventures in Wonderland* for the first time, even though I know sentences from it by heart. When you are eighteen, you will organize a class party at Hunter College with "Alice In Wonderland" as a theme.

After Alice tumbles down a rabbit hole and becomes first very small and then very tall, she remarks, "How queer everything is to-day! And yesterday things went on just as usual. I wonder if I've been changed in the night? Let me think: *was* I the same when I got up this morning? I almost think I can remember feeling a little different. But if I'm not the same, the next question is 'Who in the world am I?' Ah, *that's* the great puzzle! . . . Who am I, then? Tell me that first, and then, if I like being that person, I'll come up: if not, I'll stay down here till I'm somebody else." [8]

In the summer of 1926, Alice, did you feel "a little different," smaller and bigger by turns? Did you ask yourself, "Who am I, then?" Did you stay down in that hole till you became somebody else?

It comes home to me that *Alice in Wonderland* was not written for children.

July 2, 1996

Dear Alice Parson,

In *Through the Looking-Glass,* the White Queen says to Alice, "living backwards . . . always makes one a little giddy . . . but there's one great advantage in it, that one's memory works both ways." [9] Octavio Paz writes in *The Labyrinth of Solitude:* "Our deaths illuminate our lives. . . . Tell me how you die and I will tell you who you are." [10] I know you, Alice. I was there as your life was illuminated. My memory works both ways.

July 4, 1996

Dear Alice Parson,

A tornado tore though two nearby Connecticut towns and took the roof off a school.

This evening the sky turned a provocative blue, the wind died down, and a gentle rain began to fall. Now the sky is dark and the air is warmer. For an hour the distant boom of firecrackers interrupts my reading, so I come to the open window. Voices from other open windows and the scent of the great linden tree below enter the living room. But there is nothing to see in the night sky.

On August 4, 1926, you wrote in your diary, "we decided to go to see the Fireworks. As usual we came just in time to see nothing."

I don't really mind missing the fireworks except that I had wanted to share them with you. What I'm sharing with you, instead, Alice, is coming "just in time to see nothing."

July 6, 1996

Dear Alice Parson,

You wrote Rose, and you received your own letter back. What would you write if you were to answer my letters?

You might tell me that my reading your diary is impertinent and you don't like it at all. You might tell me that my questions and guesses are intrusive, that my speculations about you and your family are violations of the privacy your mother preserved in her life and you tried to preserve in your own. You might even be appalled at my wished-for friendship with you, extremely uninterested in the adolescent who emerges in my diaries, and put off by an adult who has just got around to reading *Alice in Wonderland*.

But you are thoughtful and intelligent and kindhearted, and I think you would be touched by someone so touched by you. You would appreciate the effort of my imagining you, your existence. You would even appreciate my imagining your rejection of this effort.

Certainly you wrote your diary for the Alice you were, whom I didn't know, and perhaps also for the Alice you will be, whom I did know. But you never destroyed your diary or asked that it be discarded. You must have known your daughter would find it, and, having found it, read it.

Perhaps, after so long a silence, your diary is the letter you are writing me, answering letters I have not yet written to you. Perhaps I had to step through the looking-glass.

Dear Alice Parson,

Two years ago in a dream my mother said to me, "You should say goodbye at the boundary." I didn't know what she meant, but I wrote down the words and the date, February 21, 1994.

A few moments after my mother's death, the young woman from Sierra Leone whom I had just hired to take care of her said, "Your mother will make a way." I didn't know what she meant, but I wrote down the words.

No one speaks for you and you do not appear in my dreams. I have just met you. I don't know how to say goodbye. I haven't found the boundary.

Wed.   Sept. 8th [1926]

Rudy owed Will $5.00. Will said that Rudy'd have to pay for 3 tickets to some show instead of paying him back. (It's rather doubtful if he'd get it back anyway).

So to-day was *the* day. We went to see 'Laff That Off' and I enjoyed myself thoroughly as, I think, did Ru and Will. It was a comedy mixed with pathos.

Thurs.   Sept. 9th

of paying him back. (Its
rather doubtful if he'd
get it back anyway).
    So to-day was the day.
We went to see Laff That Off
and I enjoyed myself
thoroughly as, I think,
did Ru and Will. It was
a comedy mixed with Pathos.

Thurs.   Sept. 9th

Alice Parson's Diary: Last Page.

PART 4

Listening

Grief does not expire like a candle
or the beacon on a lighthouse.
It simply changes temperature.
—Adam Rapp, *Nocturne*

Monday, June 30, 1997: New York City

My father died today in the morning, fifteen years ago. I still awake in disbelief.

The phone is a foot away from the bed, the number is in my head, but I am too sane to dial it. Still, I can see him. He smiles slowly. But I cannot hear his voice.

I dreamed of my mother twice last week—sad dreams, filled with her sickness. At the crucial moment in each dream, I moved my lips but could not hear myself speak.

How many voices have I lost?

Tuesday, July 1

It's been over forty years since I wrote a diary.

Writing, I listen to what haunts the writing.

Wednesday, July 2

I have been reading *The Tibetan Book of the Dead*. The ear is the organ of revelation; listening, one receives instructions about passing out of the world forever or returning to it. The final transformation, never described, is past the reach of language. Even if the one spoken to is dead, the speaking continues. The voice does not fail, even if language does.

Thursday, July 3

In early July 1990, I prepared notes for my first meeting with a social worker in New Haven. I saw her three or four times before a phone call from the Arlington Hospital collided with a scheduled appointment. I never saw her again.

I reread these notes for the first time since I wrote them. I am explaining why I have made this appointment: "When I called last week, I had had the thought that if my mother were to die, as she will, my life would break in two. . . . The loss of my mother seems unbearable. *The pain of it is something I fear I cannot bear up under.* And yet people, women, lose their mothers every day."

All this I seem to remember. But the next sentences I have completely forgotten writing.

What I most fear to lose is somehow my mother's voice— and the knowledge that she is somewhere living on this earth, in her own person and being, not just inside my head or others' memories. I have spoken to her in Virginia practically every night since she became a widow.

If I were told she could live another 10 years, on the condition I could never see her but could speak to her, I think I could bear that.

Friday, July 4: New Haven

The whole family watched fireworks on the Fourth of July four days after Dad died. We stood in a field in Virginia. There were many children the age of my two nephews. I watched my mother's eyes, open wide, gazing at the sky.

At lunch yesterday in New Haven, two friends said that as we get older life is more complicated, death simpler. I said nothing.

Saturday, July 5

We have a thirty-year-old, black-and-white television, inherited from David's grandfather. At the end of the evening news last night, behind the credits, we saw images of New York City's fireworks. There were no signs of the city below, only the sounds and calligraphy of fireworks appearing and disappearing in the night sky. Fireworks without color: absurd and miraculous. I was stunned, then strangely comforted.

Sunday, July 6

It is very late. We turn out the lights. Suddenly my eyes are wet. I remember a day ten summers ago when my mother and I, driving down a country road in Virginia, stopped at a roadside stand to buy peaches and corn. It was a tiny, unplanned detour, full of easy joys: touching and smelling the just-ripe peaches, unpeeling husks to check the white-yellow rows of Silver Queen corn—sensations that heighten our anticipation of that evening's dinner, farm-fresh.

How simple was the relation of present and future; how inevitable seemed the return of shared summer pleasures.

David holds me tightly until we fall asleep.

Monday, July 7

The large linden tree is blooming again. Its sweetness bursts through the open window.

Tuesday, July 8

Natalie is visiting from Santa Fe on her way to a funeral ceremony for her youngest brother in Mt. Desert, Maine.

Twice, late at night, a bat has appeared in the room where she sleeps. She persuaded it to exit by opening a window. Today I have searched the ceiling and walls for holes through which the bat could have entered from the attic. I find none. And yet the bat did enter, appear, leave safely, and return. Or perhaps a second bat arrived, through another crack.

I think about these invisible openings, the entry from above, the visitation and departure, the return, the new departure. I still cannot find the point of entry.

So far no new bats have appeared.

Wednesday, July 9

A small roving apparatus named Sojourner has been investigating the rocks on Mars for several days.

I can't see it, but it must be out there now, hard at work, transmitting images. No humans have accompanied Sojourner on its brave journey to the edges of human knowledge. Earth receives Sojourner's messages; the hourly radio news reports its activities; images of its sightings appear on television and the front pages of newspapers.

Astronomers are ecstatic. "This is one of the most stunning things I've ever seen, one of the great hallmarks of our time." "We've landed on Mars. We're living our dreams." Scientists are playing music to "wake up" the little rover. They give names like

Yogi and Barnacle Bill to Martian rocks. A new creation story is unfolding 119 million miles away.

Will Sojourner find evidence of any life that we can recognize, or that could have recognized us?

After my father's funeral I gazed at the earth and sky, not knowing where to look. Fifteen years later I still don't know where to look.

This little apparatus diligently searches beyond where I can see. So far it has found crusts left by the drying of salt water, "a teardrop shape," the site of ancient disaster, billions of years ago on a red planet.

Friday, July 11: Cape Cod

At midnight, after dinner in Provincetown, David and I strolled down the main street with two friends. A woman was sweeping up the remains of a broken wineglass on the pavement; behind her, four men stood staring at a bright planet in the sky. It couldn't be Venus, one man explained, quite convincingly. It might be Mars, suggested another. We and the woman who had finished sweeping assumed the stance of the four watchers.

The brightness in the sky was steady, unflickering.

I wished that Sojourner could see us on earth. I wished that it could send us signs of life.

Saturday, July 12: New Haven

There has been an accident on Mars.

The twenty-three-pound rover bumped into a three-foot-long rock whose chemical content it had been investigating with an alpha proton X-ray spectrometer. It is unharmed.

Sojourner has an expected minimum life span of seven days. Nine days have passed and it continues its voyage. If it does not again become too attached to what it studies, it may go on to its next destination.

Accidents and miracles in the sky.

Sunday, July 13

Reading Faulkner's *The Unvanquished* tonight, I came upon the young narrator's discovery of his dead granny: "She had looked little alive, but now she looked like she had collapsed, like she had been made out of a lot of little thin dry light sticks notched together and braced with cord, and now the cord had broken and all the little sticks had collapsed in a quiet heap on the floor, and somebody had spread a clean and faded calico dress over them." [1]

I think of your death. But for an hour, after all the tubes were taken out, your blue eyes were so blue and your warm hand so warm that all your life returned, and that was all I saw.

Monday, July 14

This morning I dreamed of you. In my dream, we have just finished lunch and, reversing our usual practice, you calculated the tip and I paid. We were to meet my brother, and I parked the car on a large university campus. I left you on a tree-lined street while I walked to a low building nearby. Returning, I could not find the place where I had left you. Hours passed. Two students joined in the search; we stole a car but couldn't find a map. Finally, the students abandoned the search, taking the car with them.

I wondered what you thought had happened to me. I imagined your patience as you waited for my return. I knew you knew I would find my way eventually.

When I awake, your presence lingers over the whole day.

Monday, July 14, late at night

Franz Kafka writes (in a letter), "Encounters in letters . . . are like two people separated by a sea making ripples from opposite shores." [2] I am no longer writing letters, but I still listen for the ripples from the opposite shore.

Tuesday, July 15

There are fascinating accounts of "driving" on Mars. Sojourner's "driver" on Earth first studies the Martian landscape on the monitor at his desk in Pasadena, then rehearses with a virtual rover several different routes to the same destination (a particular rock). There is an eleven-minute lag between the sending of instructions, a set of computer codes, and their arrival on Mars. This intricate communication, with its coded messages and gaps, seems a kind of interplanetary echolocation.

It is reported that the driver on Earth performs his work "while the rover is asleep" and then sleeps "while the rover is driving." Sojourner can refuse any instruction it receives.

So who is driving on Mars?

Wednesday, July 16

Yesterday David made a day trip to Manhattan to join a group tour of the streets and buildings between West Eighty-sixth and West Ninety-first near West End Avenue. The two-hour tour was conducted by a red-haired historian of architecture. (Several people actually lived in the buildings they were touring.) On his return, David remarked that his "whole childhood runs between Eighty-second and Ninety-second streets."

The tour group learned about carved limestone and shaped clay ornaments, and in which decades these materials were most plentiful; about a railroad that used to run near Riverside Park; about vanished row houses with ten-year "covenants" that established a period after which row houses could be replaced by high-rise apartments; about affinities in the designs of Central Park and Riverside Park, semibucolic sites coveted by New Yorkers who prefer nature with a skyline; about particular restrictions on the height of Upper West Side buildings (one and a half times the width of the street).

Altogether, these facts, David told me, reconfigured what had seemed immemorial, his childhood neighborhood, into "a slow-moving event." When I asked if he wanted now to tour other parts of Manhattan, he said he had learned what he needed to learn.

Twenty-five New Yorkers gather in 96 degree heat to walk and study slowly five blocks on the Upper West Side of a city they may have known all their lives. Somehow it seems a project similar to my own.

Thursday, July 17

Natalie returned last night. She told me about the ceremony she created for her brother's burial. Candles were lit, flowers brought to the gravesite. Using a single shovel, adults and children placed dirt over the deerskin pouch one brother had made the day before to hold Andrew's ashes. The leave-taking, adapted from Navajo ritual, was a procession during which none of the mourners was allowed to look back. The eldest, an aunt, had been given a broom. Following the others, she swept away their footprints, and her own, from the little path that led to the grave. The Navajos, Natalie says, would have burned everything belonging to the deceased.

Afterwards a roll of undeveloped film and a journal written in a private code were found among her brother's belongings.

After they swept clean the path, did the Navajos not look back?

Thursday, July 17, evening

The air is stale, heavy, still. The linden tree's scent has vanished. The moon is almost full.

Friday, July 18

In a dream early this morning, I am teaching one of my dramatic literature classes on a train. The students and I are eating dinner together, seated in adjoining cars, while I listen to their oral presentations. We do not finish by the end of the class period. I have scheduled one more class but cannot find a calendar. You are on the train and try to help me. It is a simple enough task to find the date for one last Monday meeting, but even with your help I cannot seem to manage it.

Awake, I look at the calendar in our bedroom. August 25, the anniversary of your death, is the last Monday in August.

Friday, July 18, early evening

This afternoon, as we were leaving for the beach, there was sudden thunder and lightning and a hailstorm of violent proportions. Even David, who doesn't usually share my interest in weather, watched what was happening to a sultry sunlit day.

As hail bounced off the windowsills and the sidewalks overflowed, my mind went back to late summer afternoon hailstorms beating against the wide glass door of the house in Virginia. And then I remembered that you told me not to be afraid if, in your dying, you were to call me "Mother." I was not to think you didn't know who I was; you would know I was not the one you were calling to.

The rain and hail ended, the sun came back, sheets of steam rose up from the pavements. The storm had become a dream.

Saturday, July 19

In a just-published poem, Frank Bidart addresses someone who is dead: *"when I hear your voice there is now / no direction in which to turn."*[3] I read these lines over and over.

Sunday, July 20

This morning as I awake, someone is vanishing from the edges of a dream I do not remember. I think it is you, but I can't be sure.

Monday, July 21

I awaken with nothing to say.

Tuesday, July 22

Late last night we watched a 1951 Bette Davis movie, *Payment on Demand*. At 4 A.M. the phone rang. The caller waited to hear my voice on the answering machine but left no message.

I wake up, listening.

Friday, July 25

Sojourner, still studying the Ares Vallis floodplain of Mars, has disappeared from the front pages. The nightly news is occupied with the suicide yesterday of serial killer Andrew Cunanan whose last and most celebrated victim was high-fashion designer Gianni Versace, shot to death as he was entering his Miami Beach mansion, Casa Casuarina, after buying a handful of weekly magazines, including the ones that later report the circumstances of his murder.

A tiny robot in outer space is already old news.

Friday, July 25, evening

I arrived early at a restaurant on the Long Island Sound where I was meeting a colleague for a drink and, naturally, headed for the ladies room. As I approached the first stall, a middle-aged woman standing a few feet to my left gestured me away. The door to the stall was slightly open, and now I heard the unseen occupant's voice in dialogue with the woman who had gestured to me. Difficulties were discussed, suggestions offered, details both mysterious and familiar presented for consideration. A woman in a wheelchair emerged from the stall and appeared at the sink next to me. The dialogue continued. Again I heard the patient instructions and this time saw the tentative attempts to follow them. I made an effort not to stare at the woman beside me, but I glimpsed a wrinkled face, shockingly youthful brown curly hair, and a forearm bruised black and blue. Her voice was wavering, loud, a little too loud.

Later, on my way to make a phone call, I saw them both waiting at the front entrance of the restaurant, silently.

Today the scene comes back, and with it a recognition of what I had observed: a wig, an elderly arm bruised by attempts to find a willing vein in a patient undergoing chemotherapy, the companion a nurse or perhaps a daughter.

Once, at a resort in Tidewater Virginia, the summer before your death, we sat on a veranda watching the sun set. Next to us was a lovely silver-haired woman, full of joy and, it seemed, health, seated in a wheelchair, smiling. I looked at her; she saw me, her smile reflecting my own. You did not look or smile.

Later, when I urged you to make wheelchair outings, I always had that Tidewater lady in mind, not a woman whose private difficulties had to be negotiated audibly in a public bathroom. But when I try to remember, I realize that you knew the difference.

In *The English Patient,* Michael Ondaatje writes, "Death means you are in the third person"[4]—a *she,* not a *you.* Writing myself, have I addressed you in the second person, again?

Saturday, July 26

Today I called a friend in New York who has recently published a book on Shakespeare. I greeted her playfully; there was a pause; then Irene said, "I must tell you that my mother just died."

Irene is older than I am and her mother died at the age of 101, but in her voice I hear my own when I was young in mourning, a voice so faraway and so close.

Sunday, July 27

A poem by Marya Bradley begins:

> White at the window;
> too late for leaves.
> But still
> still.[5]

Responding to it, David writes, "This poem, apparently about a winter scene glimpsed through a window, seems finally to be about representation and what it represents. . . . The phrasing continually suggests language's secondariness to the immediacy it would represent."

The scene of loss I write about is never seen in my writing. Even the scene outside my window remains outside my window.

Monday, July 28

The phone rings early this morning. No message.

Tuesday, July 29: New York

In New York the phone rings early in the morning, at the same hour as in New Haven yesterday. Again there is no message, but David says he thought he heard, for a few seconds, a kind of "background roar."

Who is calling?

Tuesday, July 29, midnight

This afternoon at the Museum of Modern Art we saw Ingmar Bergman's film *Cries and Whispers,* for the second time. Toward the end of the film there is an extraordinary scene. I take out a pen and write down what I see and hear on the back of the program in my lap.

The servant, Anna, says that she hears someone crying endlessly. Agnes, laid out for burial, says that she is dead, that she can't get to sleep, that she wants her sisters to come to her to warm her. The two sisters return, but are terrified by the animated corpse. Anna alone remains. She cradles and nurses Agnes at her naked breast. After the funeral and departure of the sisters and their husbands, Anna reads in Agnes's diary a record of a day in which the physical presence of Agnes's sisters made her feel a perfection of happiness. And the cries and whispers end.

What I have just described is a reconstruction from memory. When the lights come on in the theater, the sheet of paper in my lap is blank. My writing has disappeared. Later David points out that this sometimes happens with inexpensive ballpoint pens. But for a long time that blank page haunts me.

Wednesday, July 30

Through the open window I hear the rumble and swish of traffic, two men arguing, a dog barking, laughter of children, the high-pitched sound of a drill, and the low, steady, patient beat of a hammer. I fall back asleep as the city wakes.

The phone rings twice again early this morning. The second time, David answers it, listens briefly, and says, "Not interested." I didn't ask him. I have no interest, this morning, in what it is we are not interested in.

Thursday, July 31

This morning the sound of the hammering on the street is relentless: it stops my mind.

I don't mind.

Thursday, July 31, late evening

We make love in the heat of the afternoon. Our body fluids join. Afterwards we oversleep, dress quickly, and walk downtown to see a double feature of "Killer B" movies in Soho: *Shockproof* and *Scandal Sheet*.

That night in the shower, washing everything away brings everything back.

Friday, August 1

The phone rings early this morning. I answer but there is no sound, not even a dial tone.

My voice is heard but I hear nothing.

Saturday, August 2

The day after his beloved five-year-old son died, Ralph Waldo Emerson merely records in his journal the time of death: fifteen minutes past eight in the evening. I read Emerson's entry two days later. He mourns like Cleopatra: "What he looked upon is better, what he looked not upon is insignificant. . . . The sun went up the morning sky with all his light, but the landscape was dishonored by this loss." Or Lear: "Every tramper that ever tramped is abroad but the little feet are still." [6] In his essay "Experience," Emerson writes, "The only thing grief has taught me is to know how shallow it is. . . . In the death of my son, now more than two years ago, I seem to have lost a beautiful estate—no more. I cannot get it nearer to me. . . . I grieve that grief can teach me nothing. . . ." [7]

Fifteen years after his son's death, Emerson writes on July 8, 1857, that he "had the remains of my mother & of my son Waldo removed . . . to my new lot in 'Sleepy Hollow.' " The man who has said that grief can teach him nothing tells us he "ventured to look into the coffin" of his son before it was placed, with that of his mother, in a new vault covered with two slabs of granite.

He dares to look into one coffin, and says nothing. Does he not dare to look into the other?

Tuesday, August 5: New Haven

So much life, unrecorded, in the ellipses of these pages, these past few days.

Now I know how the writer of that box of letters, the author of that young girl's diary, could let so much life pass untold.

I needed to know that.

Wednesday, August 6: Watch Hill

On Wednesday, August 4, 1926, Alice Parson wrote in her diary: "So we took a walk and kept on walking."

David and I spend the afternoon walking on a Rhode Island beach. We walk for miles, looking for piping plovers who nest here on the dunes, a bird sanctuary. The sky darkens, we hear distant thunder, and two plovers appear suddenly, side by side, above our heads, fly out over the ocean, make a figure eight, still side by side, and return to the dunes behind us. Then we see half a dozen more of them, flying together over the water and returning to hidden sites on shore. It is a dramatic appearance and disappearance. What we walk toward has arrived as if on cue, but with the jarring force of the unknowable.

Friday, August 8: New Haven

Emerson, who writes more than three million words in journals and miscellaneous notebooks, says, "There is always a residuum unknown, unanalysable."

Saturday, August 9

Three glowing officials present their first month's report on what they call a 100 percent successful space mission to Mars. Sojourner has circumnavigated the mother craft, Pathfinder, twice, once clockwise and once counterclockwise, and is now heading for higher ground. The goal is "exploration: to get to the top of the hill, look over the edge," and still maintain contact with its mother.

The little rover has greatly extended its predicted working life, but the mother craft is slowing down. Scientists are trying to extend her lifetime. Since battery capacity will degenerate over time, Pathfinder will go into "hibernation mode," losing her memory at night. Every fifth day she will stay awake all night.

Sunday, August 10

I am awakened by the stuttering of the fire alarm in our apartment building. There is no smell of smoke. Ten minutes later, I hear a fire engine. It is going somewhere else.

I am fully awake. I think of fires I have known. I remember one summer when I was thirteen: as I bend over the stove in the kitchen, my thin summer pajama top catches fire. Before I am fully aware of what has happened, my father tears off the burning garment. I remember my embarrassment at being half-naked in his presence, and then, much later, my shame at feeling embarrassment instead of gratitude. He saved me from disfigurement, perhaps he saved my life.

When he was dying, I taught my father to smoke marijuana in an attempt to relieve the nausea of chemotherapy. I bought him an elegant wall clock with large numbers so he could read it from anywhere in "the new room" where he died. I held his hand, so comforting in its warmth, on good days when he seemed to want my silent company. I never saved his life.

Monday, August 11

Yesterday David found a version of Bergman's *Cries and Whispers*[8] in a yellowing, coffee-stained, October 21, 1972, *New Yorker* he had saved. Agnes is thirty-seven and has cancer of the womb. Anna had a daughter who died at the age of three. I reread the ending.

The servant, Anna, hears "despairing, childish sobs" that stop when she enters the bedroom where Agnes's corpse lies.

> Anna sees that the dead woman has been crying. . . . Agnes'
> lips begin to move and then she speaks in a faraway voice,
> which is changed and laborious, infinitely weary:
> —Are you afraid of me now? she asks. Anna shakes her
> head. No, she's not afraid.
> —I am dead, you see, Agnes says. . . .
> —The trouble is, I can't get to sleep. I can't leave all of
> you. . . . Can't anyone help me? she moans. I'm so tired.
> —It's only a dream, Anna whispers in a flash of inspiration.
> —No, it's not a dream, Agnes answers tormentedly. For
> you, perhaps it's a dream. But not for me.

After Agnes's funeral, Anna listens: "Faintly, very far away and scarcely discernible, she hears the child's crying." The crying is the crying of the daughter to the mother. Anna, left alone in the house, carefully opens Agnes's diary. We see Agnes's handwriting and then Anna reads aloud from the diary: "And I feel a great gratitude to my life, which gives me so much." In the film, there is irony in the contrast between the wholesome words on the soundtrack and the visual image of the diarist's face, strained by illness. But, at the end, when writing tells the story, weeping stops.

Wednesday, August 13

Today, in preparation for a book I am writing on playwrights in rehearsal, I was to begin observing the New York production of Arthur Miller's *The American Clock,* a play about a Jewish family living in Brooklyn during the Depression. But rehearsals have been postponed until September. So I fill myself up with Miller: his one-act plays, his autobiographical memoir *Timebends,* hundreds of his published interviews and conversations. In a 1977 interview, I find him saying, "I don't think my life is of any interest as such. . . . It's where you can see something like the human situation. . . . Whether there's any light thrown, so that one comes away from it somehow a little heavier than he went into it."[9]

The one who first comes away from the writing a little heavier is the writer, I am learning.

Thursday, August 14

In a novel by Ivy Compton-Burnett, one character says after the mother has died, "The blank is all that is left."[10] The blank is not all that is left. The blank that is left is not blank.

Friday, August 15

I am awakened by the sound of my brother's voice being recorded on the answering machine: "This is Ken, calling to try to figure out where you're going to be on the 25th of August." He is driving his son Robert back to Providence to begin his junior year at Brown, and he and I will try to meet in New Haven on August 25. Neither of us mentions that this is the anniversary of our mother's death.

Saturday, August 16: Ashfield

I am watching rehearsals of Jean-Claude van Itallie's play *The Ti-betan Book of the Dead, or How Not to Do It Again*, at the director's farmhouse in Ashfield, Massachusetts, where fourteen adults, three children, two dogs, a white rabbit, and four Polish laying hens (all named Murray) are living communally this month. It is my inten-tion to remain as invisible as possible.

I sit in darkness as actors move about me, improvising in the upper rooms of a nineteenth-century barn. I listen and write. When there is silence, I listen and continue to write.

Sunday, August 17

Before evening rehearsals begin, the director, Kim Mancuso, in-vites the company out to the meadow to gaze at a nearly full moon; a wall of mist advances from the trees around us as bats whirl shakily above our heads.

What I thought was a diversion is a fuller taking in of the scene, another kind of noticing.

Monday, August 18

I am looking at my brother's favorite photo of our family, the one he keeps in his wallet, taken at Port Jervis, New York, on the Del-aware River. There are two versions of this photograph, one taken by my brother and one taken by me. In each photo one of us is miss-ing. The others are posed on or behind a large rock that, Dad pointed out, marks the site where three states meet: New York, New Jersey, and Pennsylvania. This summer my brother mentions that we needed to pass through a cemetery to find that boundary-defying rock. This photo is finally beginning to interest me.

Tuesday, August 19: New Haven

David has been in New York for a week writing a new play. When he returns, he brings me a tiny newspaper clipping headlined "NASA Loses Contact with Its Mars Rover." Communication between scientists on Earth and Sojourner on Mars was "cut off" on Saturday and no one is able to explain the "breakdown."

I am upset: the rover, working so hard to communicate, is now lost. David smiles: the rover isn't lost; it is now simply exploring on its own.

I remember our conversation four summers ago about the baby bat immobilized on the second-floor landing of our apartment building. Then, too, he took the more hopeful view. This time maybe he's right.

I look up "contact" in my dictionary. In reference to electricity, it is a device that makes or breaks a connection between two conductors. Contact can rupture conductivity. My eye falls on the definition of conduction: the transmission or conveying of something through a medium or passage, especially without perceptible motion of the medium itself. I sit very still.

Wednesday, August 20

In the August 25, 1997, issue of *Time,* Barbara Ehrenreich identifies the sex of Sojourner: "(yes, the robot is a girl)." I hear nothing further about human contact with her.

Thursday, August 21

It rained all night. This morning I lie in bed, eyes closed, listening to the fierce wind outside.

Friday, August 22

It surprises me: boundary lines that once seemed necessary, even desirable, now shift, change, disappear.

Saturday, August 23

My brother calls. We discover that I may miss him as he drives through Connecticut on August 25th. I listen to his voice. We meet there.

Sunday, August 24

I look for signs of your presence in the world, and I find them everywhere, even in enormous change, which you, and I, had feared.

Monday, August 25

Afterword

Darling Mom,

Near the outdoor amphitheater in Arlington whose activities you publicized and attended, a bench has been installed. It is the first in Lubber Run Park to have a plaque. The bench is already weather-worn, the gold plaque slightly scratched, by the time I first visit it. (You would say, *Of course; it's meant to be used.*)

It sits by tall trees that border a curve in the bubbling stream that runs the length of the park where we used to walk and picnic and abuts the building where you once worked. On the plaque is a quote that I chose from Wordsworth's poem "Nutting":

> . . . with gentle hand
> Touch—for there is a spirit in the woods.[1]

On the path in front of the bench someone has playfully spray painted the words, "THE ROCK," with two arrows pointing toward a large stone on the other side of the stream. My gaze passes over the stream to the large stone. There, in the same white spray paint, I see some deliberate, barely legible child's writing that will disappear before my next visit.

When you speak from your bench, who is listening?
I am, now.

Notes

Part 1. Echolocations

Epigraph, part 1: poem written in a letter quoted in *New Poems of Emily Dickinson,* ed. William H. Shurr with Anna Dunlap and Emily Grey Shurr (Chapel Hill: Univ. of North Carolina Press, 1993), 6. Printed as Poem #1639 in *The Complete Works of Emily Dickinson,* ed. Thomas H. Johnson (Boston: Little, Brown and Co., 1960), 672.

1. William Trevor, "Field of Battle," *New Yorker,* May 17, 1993, 84.

2. William Shakespeare, *King Lear:* 5.3.307–8. *The Riverside Shakespeare,* ed. G. Blakemore Evans, 2nd ed. (Boston: Houghton Mifflin, 1997), 1192.

3. Sappho, Poem #87, in Mary Barnard, *Sappho: A New Translation* (Berkeley: Univ. of California Press, 1958), n.p.

4. Goethe quoted by Ludwig Wittgenstein in *Remarks on the Philosophy of Psychology,* vol. 1, ed. G. E. M. Anscombe and G. H. Von Wright (Chicago: Univ. of Chicago Press, 1980), #889, 157e.

5. John Keats, "The Fall of Hyperion. A Dream," in *John Keats: The Complete Poems,* ed. John Barnard, 3rd ed. (New York: Penguin, 1988), 1.163, p. 439.

6. William Wordsworth, "Ode: Intimations of Immortality from Recollections of Early Childhood," in *The Poetical Works of Wordsworth,* ed. Thomas Hutchinson (New York: Oxford Univ. Press, 1960), 11.206–7, p. 462.

7. Virgil, *The Aeneid,* in *The Aeneid of Virgil, Books 1–6,* ed. R. D. Williams (New York: St. Martin's, 1992), book 1, 1.462, p. 15.

8. Beverly Mack, letter to author, June 1993.

Part 2. Two Voices

1. Joyce Carol Oates, "The One Unforgivable Sin," *New York Times Book Review,* July 25, 1993, 25.

2. Trevor, "Field of Battle," 84.

3. Milton Moss, letter to author, September 7, 1994.

4. Diane Arbus quoted by Michael Sprinker, "Fictions of the Self: The End of Autobiography," in *Autobiography: Essays Theoretical and Critical,* ed. James Olney (Princeton: Princeton Univ. Press, 1980), 321.

5. Alice P. Letzler, "Parents' Guide to Successful Conferences," Arlington County Public Schools, Arlington, Virginia, 1952, 7, 8, 6, 11.

6. Marianne Moore, "Armour's Undermining Modesty," in *The Complete Poems of Marianne Moore* (New York: Penguin, 1981), 152.

7. *New York Times,* July 31, 2005, N1, N22.

8. Alice P. Letzler, "The Importance of Citizen Participation in School Planning," speech delivered to Bellevue Forest Citizens' Association, June 7, 1962.

Part 3. Summer 1926 & Summer 1996

Epigraph, part 3: Kierkegaard quoted in *Maps,* a Somali novel by Nuruddin Farah (New York: Pantheon, 1986), 117.

1. Dr. William Parson, letter to author, June 4, 1996.

2. Lucille "Buffy" Parson, letter to author, June 4, 1996.

3. Buffy Parson, Dr. William Parson, letters to author, June 4, 1996.

4. Kathleen Woodward, *Aging and Its Discontents: Freud and Other Fictions* (Bloomington: Indiana Univ. Press, 1991), 119.

5. Eavan Boland, "Domestic Interior," section 11 in *Collected Poems* (Manchester, UK: Carcanet, 1995), 98.

6. *Laird and Lee's Vest-Pocket Webster Pronouncing Dictionary Including Leading Synonyms* (Chicago: Laird and Lee, 1921), 5.

7. Milton Moss, letter to author, September 7, 1994.

8. Lewis Carroll, *Alice's Adventures in Wonderland and Through the Looking-Glass* (New York: New American Library, 1960), 26–27.

9. Carroll, *Through the Looking-Glass,* 172.

10. Octavio Paz, *The Labyrinth of Solitude: Life and Thought in Mexico* (New York: Grove, 1961), 54.

Part 4. Listening

Epigraph, part 4: Adam Rapp, *Nocturne* (New York: Faber and Faber, 2002), 79.

1. William Faulkner, *The Unvanquished* (New York: Vintage, 1966), 175.

2. Franz Kafka quoted by Leo A. Lensing in a review of *Briefe, 1900–1912,* a five-volume edition of Kafka's letters. *TLS,* October 8, 1999, 9.

3. Frank Bidart, "The Yoke," in *Desire* (New York: Farrar, Straus and Giroux, 1997), 14.

4. Michael Ondaatje, *The English Patient* (New York: Vintage, 1993), 247.

5. Marya Bradley, "White at the Window," unpublished poem.

6. Emerson's journal entries are taken from *Emerson in His Journals,* ed. Joel Porte (Cambridge: Harvard Univ. Press, 1982), 176, 476, viii.

7. Ralph Waldo Emerson, *Selected Essays,* ed. Larzer Ziff (New York: Penguin, 1982), 287–88.

8. Ingmar Bergman, *Cries and Whispers,* translated from the Swedish by Alan Blair. *New Yorker,* October 21, 1972, 60, 62, 74.

9. Arthur Miller quoted in *Conversations with Arthur Miller,* ed. Matthew C. Roudané (Jackson: Univ. Press of Mississippi, 1987), 289.

10. Ivy Compton-Burnett, *A House and Its Head* (New York: New York Review Books, 2001), 75.

Afterword

1. William Wordsworth, "Nutting," 11.55–56, p. 147.

Other titles in Writing American Women

The American Life of Ernestine L. Rose
Carol A. Kolmerten

Dear Yeats, Dear Pound, Dear Ford: Jeanne Robert Foster and Her Circle of Friends
Richard Londraville and Janis Londraville

The Dream Book: An Anthology of Writings by Italian American Women
Helen Barolini, ed.

Grandmothers: Granddaughters Remember
Marguerite Guzman Bouvard, ed.

Hattie: A Woman's Mission to Burma
Joan W. Swift

Intimate Reading: The Contemporary Women's Memoir
Janet Mason Ellerby

Martha Matilda Harper and the American Dream:
How One Woman Changed the Face of Modern Business
Jane R. Plitt

Mizora: A Prophecy
Mary E. Bradley Lane; Jean Pfaelzer, ed.